Cambridge English

SECOND EDITION

Complete First

Teacher's Book

Guy Brook-Hart

CAMBRIDGE
UNIVERSITY PRESS

University Printing House, Cambridge CB2 8BS, United Kingdom

Cambridge University Press is part of the University of Cambridge.

It furthers the University's mission by disseminating knowledge in the pursuit of education, learning and research at the highest international levels of excellence.

www.cambridge.org
Information on this title: www.cambridge.org/9781107643949

First published 2008
Second edition 2014
8th printing 2015

Printed in Dubai by Oriental Press

A catalogue record for this publication is available from the British Library

ISBN 978-1-107-63390-2 Student's Book without answers with CD-ROM
ISBN 978-1-107-65617-8 Student's Book with answers with CD-ROM
ISBN 978-1-107-64394-9 Teacher's Book with Teacher's Resources Audio CD/CD-ROM
ISBN 978-1-107-65220-0 Workbook without answers with Audio CD
ISBN 978-1-107-66339-8 Workbook with answers with Audio CD
ISBN 978-1-107-68734-9 Class Audio CDs (2)
ISBN 978-1-107-66666-5 Presentation Plus
ISBN 978-1-107-65186-9 Student's Pack (Student's Book without answers with CD-ROM, Workbook without answers with Audio CD)
ISBN 978-1-107-69835-2 Student's Book Pack (Student's Book with answers with CD-ROM with Class Audio CDs (2)

Contents

Introduction

Who *Complete First* is for

Complete First Second Edition is an enjoyable and motivating topic-based course designed to give a thorough preparation for the revised **Cambridge English: First** exam (Common European Framework of Reference level B2). It is particularly suitable for **teenagers** and **young adults**. It offers:

- stimulating **authentic reading texts**, providing training in the reading techniques and strategies needed to deal with exam reading tasks
- **listening tasks**, providing practice with strategies for handling exam listening tasks
- a systematic approach to exam **speaking tasks**, providing models for students to follow and **clear outcomes** for improved exam performance
- many opportunities for personalisation, with further speaking activities
- a step-by-step approach to writing tasks, with **models** to work from and **sample answers**
- comprehensive coverage of all **major grammar areas** tested in the **Cambridge English: First** exam. These are supported by work on correcting **common grammar mistakes** made by exam candidates, as revealed by the **Cambridge Learner Corpus**
- vocabulary input based on information from the **English Vocabulary Profile (EVP)** and the **Cambridge Learner Corpus**. The EVP, which is part of English Profile, is funded mainly by Cambridge University Press and Cambridge English Language Assessment. It aims to create a 'profile' for English linked to the Common European Framework of Reference for Languages (CEF). The EVP provides detailed information about the vocabulary that learners can be expected to use at each CEF level. For more information, please visit www.englishprofile.org.

  The CLC is part of the Cambridge English Corpus and has been developed by Cambridge English Language Assessment and Cambridge University Press to provide evidence about language use in order to produce better language-teaching materials. It contains large numbers of scripts produced by candidates in Cambridge exams. The scripts have been error coded to enable research into language areas which students at each exam level find problematic.

What the Teacher's Book contains

- **Unit notes** for the 14 units of the Student's Book which:
  - state the **objectives** of each unit
  - give **step-by-step advice** on how to treat each exercise in the unit
  - contain **information about exam tasks** and what they are testing
  - offer a wide range of suggestions for **alternative treatments** of the material in the Student's Book
  - offer a wide range of ideas for **extension activities** to follow up Student's Book activities
  - contain **comprehensive answer keys** for each activity and exercise
  - contain **complete recording scripts**. The sections of text which provide the answers to listening tasks are underlined.

- A **Teacher's Resources CD-ROM** containing:
  - **14 photocopiable activities**, one for each unit, designed to provide enjoyable recycling of work done in the Student's Book unit, but without a specific exam-style focus. Each activity is accompanied by detailed teacher's notes.
  - **14 photocopiable progress tests** which test the grammar and vocabulary taught in the units and reading comprehension skills. Each test can be given to a class to do in a lesson of 60 minutes.
  - **14 photocopiable word lists** covering vocabulary encountered in the Student's Book. The vocabulary items are accompanied by definitions supplied by corpus-informed Cambridge dictionaries. These lists can be given to students for private study, reference or revision after they have completed the unit, or for reference while they are working on the unit if you prefer. The lists are intended as an extra tool for extending students' vocabulary.
  - **photocopiable scripts** of the recorded materials used in the Listening, Speaking and Grammar sections. Unlike the scripts in the Teacher's Book, these do not have the answers underlined and so can be used for follow-up work after completing the tasks in the Student's Book.

1 A family affair

Unit objectives

- **Reading and Use of English Part 6:** introduction to task type; skimming for main idea; using referencing and subject matter to place sentences
- **Reading and Use of English Part 2:** introduction to task type; skimming for general ideas
- **Writing Part 1:** introduction to task type; planning and writing an essay; expressing personal opinions; using *although, however, on the other hand* and *whereas*
- **Listening Part 1:** introduction to task type; identifying key ideas in questions; listening for gist and for specific information; asking questions
- **Speaking Part 1:** introduction to task type; giving personal information and personal opinions; giving extended answers
- **Pronunciation:** word stress (1)
- **Vocabulary:** phrasal verbs, e.g. *get on with, do up*, etc.; adjectives describing personality and behaviour; collocations describing housework; collocations with *make* and *do*; phrases to describe districts and neighbourhoods
- **Grammar:** contrasting present perfect simple and continuous

Starting off

As a warmer With books closed, ask students to note down three activities they do with their family. In pairs, they should compare their activities and say why and when they do them.

Extension idea Ask students: *How important is family life in your country?*

Listening | Part 1

1 ***As a warmer*** Go through the Exam information box with students. Tell them that each piece is quite short and lasts about 30 seconds.

This part tests students' ability to understand gist, detail, function, purpose, attitude, opinion, etc. Tell students that in the exam there will be no relationship of subject matter between the different extracts.

Elicit that it is important to underline the key idea in the questions because it helps students to focus on what they should be listening for. Tell them not to underline the key ideas in the alternatives A–C because the different ideas may confuse them while listening.

Suggested underlining
2 doing to the house **3** How often, do sporting activities, father **4** family celebrations, feel
5 sister, annoyed **6** tired **7** message, mother
8 chose, trumpet

2 Tell students:

- not to choose an option until they have heard the whole piece
- to listen for specific words and phrases which give them the answer
- to listen the second time to check their answers.

Alternative treatment Play the first piece only. Then elicit the correct answer from students and the words they heard which gave them the answer (*I suspect she finds explaining algebra and things quite fun …*). Point out that the words in the answer (*she enjoys it*) will probably not be the same as the words students hear.

To break up the listening activity, you can round up after, say, question 4. To do this, ask students to work in pairs and compare their answers before rounding up with the whole class.

Answers
1 A **2** B **3** C **4** A **5** A **6** B **7** C **8** C

Note: The words/sentences which give answers to questions in the main listening exercises are numbered and underlined in the scripts for easy reference.

CD 1 Track 02

Presenter: One. You hear part of a conversation with a boy called Patrick.

Friend: Do you help much around the house then, Patrick?

Patrick: Not much. I make my bed and occasionally do the washing-up, but I'm studying pretty hard for my exams at the moment, so my mum ends up doing most of the housework while I get on with my studying. Even so, she still finds time to give me a hand with my studies from time to time. She used to be a maths teacher and she knows I'm getting a bit nervous about the maths exam.' [1]I suspect she finds explaining algebra and things quite fun, and actually she's pretty good at it, too.

Presenter: Two. You hear a girl called Tracey talking to a friend.

Friend: So, how often do you all do things together as a family then, Tracey?

Tracey: Oh, all the time, I mean at least once a week, at weekends. You see, we live in this really old house which we've been working on together. In fact, we've just finished doing up the kitchen. It's been great fun because we've all been doing it together. We made a lot of mess, of course, which we had to clear up, and [2]now we're decorating it, so it's looking nicer and nicer. We had lots of really big arguments about the colour, but in the end, I got my way.

Presenter: Three. You hear a girl called Vicky taking part in a class discussion.

Teacher: Does anyone ever do sports with other people in their family? Yes, Vicky …

Vicky: Well, my dad's a fitness fanatic, so he's always running or cycling or doing something energetic. [3]I do sporty things with him now and again, more often in the summer though occasionally at other times of the year as well. He's got a few days' holiday at the moment, so he's probably doing something sporty right now. He's always asking me to go out cycling with him, but now I've got other things to get on with, including a new boyfriend, so recently [3]I've been spending more time with him and not so much with my dad.

Presenter: Four. You hear a boy called Kostas talking about family celebrations.

Friend: I take it you don't enjoy family celebrations then, Kostas?

Kostas: Not much, to be honest. I just feel [4]they go on for too long and I'd prefer to be out doing other things with my mates, not sitting around listening to my uncles and aunts and that. Everyone's always telling the same old jokes or singing the same old songs and I've heard them all millions of times, so I guess [4]I've just lost interest. I mean, [4]it's just not much fun any more. I try not to show it, but, you know, I just wait for things to end and then, when I get the chance, I go out with my friends. That's what I really like.

Presenter: Five. You hear a boy called Rajiv talking to his sister on the phone.

Lina: Hiya!

Rajiv: Are you still at Jasvinder's house?

Lina: Yeah, why? We're just playing some games.

Rajiv: Computer games? I've been looking for my laptop – you wouldn't have any idea what's happened to it, would you?

Lina: Oh, [5]I've just borrowed it for the evening. Hope you don't mind.

Rajiv: Oh, honestly! [5]You're always using my stuff without asking me, and I've got this really important homework project! Now what am I going to do?

Lina: Use Dad's computer instead. He won't mind.

Rajiv: Look, I can't do that – I've got everything saved on mine and you've just walked off with it.

Presenter: Six. You hear a boy called Marco talking to a friend.

Friend: Hi, Marco. What's the matter? You look exhausted!

Marco: I am! You see, we went on this family outing yesterday. My mum said it'd be good for me to have a break from all my school work – she says I've been working too hard. Anyway, we went down to the seaside, which is quite a long way, as you know, and then [6]my dad and I spent ages swimming and playing in the sea. Mum had to drive us home, [6]we were both so worn out by the time we came out!

Presenter: Seven. You hear a girl called Samin leaving a telephone message for her mother.

Samin: Hi, Mum! It's Julia's birthday today. Anyway, she's having a party, and I've been with Susana and Clare to buy her a present. We got her a really nice bag, but it was quite expensive. Anyway, [7]the reason I'm phoning you's because she's invited us to spend the night at her place. Is that all right, Mum? It is Friday night, so I don't have to get up early tomorrow or anything. I'll give you a call when I want you to come and pick me up.

Presenter: Eight. You hear an interview with a young musician called Pau.

Interviewer: Pau, you play the trumpet in the town band. Why did you go for that particular instrument?

Pau: Well, I don't think I really had a choice. [8]There've always been trumpeters in the band from my family, and my granddad gave me his when he stopped playing, so I think he'd have been shocked if I'd chosen something else. I quite like it, but I think I'd prefer the guitar because then I could play in a rock band instead. Perhaps I'll learn that as well – you don't have to just choose one instrument. You can play others as well.

Extension idea 1 Print out and photocopy the recording scripts from the Teacher's Resources CD-ROM and ask students to listen again, underlining the phrases which give the answers.

Extension idea 2 Write these headings on the board: *Giving children an education, A common project, Enjoying doing the same things, Family celebrations, Sharing, Having someone to care about you.*

Ask students in pairs to match the headings with questions 1–8, pointing out that some questions will share a heading. Then ask them to discuss: *Which aspect of family life do you think is the most important? Why?*

Extension idea 3 Ask students to look at the photo with question 8. Ask: *What photos would you put with the other questions?*

3 You may need to remind students how to form questions in the present simple. The questions contain common student mistakes.

Answers
2 How often **do** you all **do** things together as a family?
3 **Do you (ever) do/play** sports with other people in your family?
4 **Do** you enjoy family celebrations?
5 How **do** other members of the family annoy you?
6 **Do** you have / **Have** you **got** any family traditions?

4 ***Extension idea*** Ask students to change partners and report what they have discovered about the person they interviewed.

Vocabulary

Phrasal verbs

Note: All the phrasal verbs in this section are classified in the English Vocabulary Profile at B2 level. See page 4 for information about the English Profile.

1 EP ***As a warmer*** With books closed, ask students in pairs to write down three or four phrasal verbs they know. Round up with the whole class and write the verbs on the board.

Elicit example sentences containing the phrasal verbs and ask students what each one means.

Ask: *Why are phrasal verbs difficult to learn?* (**Suggested answer**: Because it is often difficult to see the relation between the parts of a phrasal verb and its meaning; particles/prepositions are difficult to remember.)

Alternative treatment If you haven't already done so, print out and distribute copies of the recording script for Listening Part 1 from the Teacher's Resources CD-ROM. Ask students to find the verbs in the script so they can see them in context.

Answers
2 f **3** d **4** b **5** e **6** a

2 **Answers**
2 worn out; clearing up **3** went on
4 pick up; do up

Extension idea Ask students in pairs to write their own example sentences for each phrasal verb.

Reading and Use of English | Part 6

1 ***As a warmer*** Ask students to look at the photos on pages 10 and 11. Ask: *What do you think these teenagers' parents would say about each of the teenagers in the photos?*

Ask students to work in small groups and make a list of four or five adjectives that parents often use about their teenage children, e.g. *untidy.*

Write their adjectives on the board. Ask them which ones are positive and which ones are negative. If there are many more of one than the other, ask them why.

Encourage students to copy useful or unfamiliar adjectives into their notebooks.

Then move on to the vocabulary exercises in the book.

Note: All the adjectives listed in this exercise are classified in the English Vocabulary Profile at B2 level.

If you wish, you can print and distribute the Unit 1 word list from the Teacher's Resources CD-ROM for students to refer to as they do this exercise.

Alternative treatment Ask students to use their dictionaries where necessary.

Answers
usually positive: concerned, enthusiastic, hard-working, mature, organised, reasonable, responsible, self-confident, understanding
usually negative: aggressive, anxious, bad-tempered, critical, impatient, impolite, unreliable
could be either: sensitive, strict

2 Go through the Language reference on page 181 with students before they do this exercise.

Answers
concerned – unconcerned
enthusiastic – unenthusiastic
mature – immature
organised – disorganised
reasonable – unreasonable
responsible – irresponsible
sensitive – insensitive

Extension idea Ask students to think of other words which begin with *dis-*, *un-*, *im-*, *ir-* and *in-*.

3 **Answers**
Student's own answers. These may depend very much on local culture.

4 To get them started, elicit a few more ideas from the whole class.

Extension idea 1 Ask: *Do you think parents and children have always had the same attitudes towards each other, or are they changing? Why?*

Extension idea 2 If your students are from different countries, ask some of these questions as appropriate:

- *How do the attitudes vary between the different nationalities in this class?*
- *Are there some things which are the same for all nationalities?*
- *Why do you think this is?*

5 Point out to students that the reading task requires them to replace missing sentences in the numbered gaps. The sentences are listed after the text. This task tests students' ability to understand:

- how texts are structured and how the information and argument of a text develops
- referencing within and around the missing sentences.

For this reason, good exam technique is to read the main body of text first, identifying the main idea of each paragraph.

Tell students that by making notes next to each paragraph, they are seeing how the text is organised and structured.

When they have finished, ask them to compare their notes in pairs.

Suggested answers
Para. 2: trust teenagers to behave responsibly
Para. 3: brain development
Para. 4: scientific findings about teenage behaviour
Para. 5: negotiation and compromise
Para. 6: concentrate on your goal

6 As this is students' first encounter with this type of task, words and phrases have been underlined in the text and in the sentences to help them identify the links between the two. Tell students that in the exam, none of the text will be underlined.

Alternative treatment Tell students that the correct answer to question 1 is G and elicit why. (Answer: The sentence says: *You're not going out looking like that, are you?* and the text follows with: *You'd never say that to an adult ...* Ask: *What would you never say to an adult? Why does it show a total lack of respect?*)

Ask students to work in pairs and decide on their answers, giving reasons for them.

Answers
1 G **2** E **3** A **4** C **5** B **6** F
D is not needed.

7 Before students start, ask them to read their roles and then discuss with the class:

- how the text says parents should react in this situation, and how they think normal parents would react in this situation
- how they personally would behave in this situation as teenagers, and whether the average teenager might behave differently.

Tell students that there are clearly different ways of playing these roles, so they can choose how to do it.

Alternative treatment Tell students they are going to do the role play twice – once where parent and teenager have a bad relationship and once where they have a good, respectful relationship.

After they have played the two situations, select one or more pairs to act out each situation in front of the whole class.

When they have finished, ask the rest of the class:

- how well each parent and each teenager handled the situation
- how realistic these parent–teenager relationships seemed to them.

Grammar

Present perfect simple and continuous

1 Ask students which sentences are present perfect simple and which are continuous. When they have done the exercise, go through the Language reference section on page 178 with them.

Answers
1 1 a, 2 b **2** 1 b, 2 a **3** 1 a, 2 b

2 Before students do the exercise, elicit why the example in question 1 is continuous (Answer: It emphasises the activity). Ask students to check their answers together in pairs and, where they disagree, discuss. Encourage them to look at the Language reference section when doing the exercise.

Answers
2 have asked **3** have cleaned **4** has been playing
5 have passed **6** has only been working
7 have spent **8** have been cooking

3 Tell students that exercises with this icon contain mistakes frequently made by candidates in the exam and that it's important to:

- pay special attention when using the present perfect to avoid these mistakes
- be able to find and correct these mistakes if they make them themselves.

Use the example in question 1 to elicit why *was* is wrong and should be replaced by *have been* (Answer: Because *since* indicates that it is something which started in the past and is still true now).

Do questions 2 and 3 with the whole class so they see what they should be doing. They can do questions 4–8 in pairs.

Answers
2 ~~learned~~ have learned / have been learning
3 ~~work~~ have worked **4** ~~play~~ have been playing
5 ~~had been doing~~ have been doing **6** ~~are~~ have been **7** ~~had been talking~~ have been talking
8 ~~dance~~ have been dancing

Reading and Use of English | Part 2

1 ***As a warmer*** With books closed, ask students to brainstorm different household tasks in small groups. Round up the activity by writing the ideas on the board, then ask students to work in their groups and say which tasks they enjoy doing, which they don't mind doing and which they hate doing, and why.

Then ask them to do the exercise in the book.

Answers
1 e **2** h **3** d **4** b **5** g **6** f **7** a **8** c

2 ***Alternative treatment*** Turn the first question into a class survey by getting students to compile details of who does each task in the family. This can then be developed into a class discussion of any surprising trends or imbalances (e.g. one member of the family doing many more of the household jobs than others), etc. This will then serve as an introduction to the next activity.

3 Reading and Use of English Part 2, the open cloze, tests students' knowledge of language structures and their understanding of the text. The words they need will either be grammatical words, such as articles, prepositions and auxiliary verbs, or lexico-grammatical words, such as linking words, parts of phrasal verbs and fixed phrases. Extensive reading outside the classroom is useful preparation for this and other parts of the exam, as it builds up students' knowledge of English.

Tell students it is important to skim the text first to get an idea of the content and argument before they deal with the questions. Give students one minute to skim the text.

Answers
For pocket money, preparation for adult life, duty to parents, because it's fair, their parents make them

4 You can help students with this type of exercise, which they will find challenging to start with, by eliciting or guiding them towards the answers, especially for the first few gaps. For the example (0):

- ask them to look at the position of the gap in the sentence and say what type of word they need (Answer: a preposition)
- elicit that the preposition is used to express purpose, i.e. why do some teenagers do housework? … pocket money.

Point out that they need to read around the gap and think about:

- the meaning of the sentence
- the type of word (preposition, auxiliary verb, etc.) that they will need for the gap.

For question 1, to guide them to the answer and to make them aware that they need to consider meaning as well as grammar, ask:

- What does *it* refer to? (Answer: doing household chores)
- What does *see* mean here? (Answer: consider/regard)
- What type of word will go between the pronoun and a noun phrase? (Answer: a preposition) Students can do questions 2–8 alone and then discuss their answers in pairs.

Don't go through all the answers until they have used the clues in Exercise 5.

Answers
1 as **2** at **3** do **4** their **5** There **6** to **7** not **8** rather

5 Ask students to improve their answers by using these clues.

6 ***Alternative treatment*** Do this activity briefly as a whole-class discussion to round off the section.

Vocabulary

Collocations with *make* and *do*

As a warmer With books closed, elicit household chores with *make* or *do*, e.g. *make the bed, do the ironing*, etc. Ask students if they can think of other phrases with *make* or *do*, e.g. *do homework, make friends*, etc.

1 ***Alternative treatment*** If everyone in the class speaks the same first language, ask them to suggest a variety of collocations in their own language with verb–noun, adjective–noun and adverb–verb.

Tell students to keep a section of their notebooks for collocations and to copy the table into their notebooks, where they should complete it.

Note: *Do an impression of someone* and *make work for someone* are also possible collocations, though not so common and not the object of this exercise.

Answers
make: an arrangement, the bed, a change, a choice, a decision, an effort, an excuse, friends, an impression, a mistake, money, a noise, a phone call, a plan, progress, a promise
do: business, the cleaning, a course, (an) exercise, a favour, homework, housework, a job, the shopping, (a) sport, work

2 Ask students to do this exercise without referring to the table from Exercise 1. When they have finished, they can then look at it to check their answers.

Answers
1 do **2** make; do **3** make; make **4** made; making **5** do; make **6** doing; do

Extension idea If you have class sets of a good learner's dictionary, ask students to look up *do* and *make* in the dictionary and find other collocations which they can then add to the table.

3 ***Alternative treatment*** Ask students to do the exercise in small groups and take turns to 'present' what they did or made to the whole group. When each student finishes, the group should ask two or three questions to find out more about what the student did or made.

Speaking | Part 1

1 ***As a warmer*** Refer students to the Exam information box at the beginning of this section. Tell them that in Part 1, the examiner asks questions about the candidates themselves, and it is often considered an opportunity to break the ice and put the candidates at their ease.

Some of the questions may be predictable to some extent, so students should ensure that they know the vocabulary to describe, for example, their studies, their interests, their family and their neighbourhood. However, they should not memorise pre-prepared answers, as the examiner will recognise these and be unable to assess them: the examiner's task is to assess the quality of spontaneous speaking.

They should avoid one-word or very short answers where possible, as they will be assessed on their ability to express themselves grammatically, fluently and with an appropriate range of vocabulary, so they should aim to use longer sentences, and often more than one sentence, to answer.

Point out that although this part of the Speaking paper may be perceived as easier than the other parts, it is assessed in the same way and so requires equally serious preparation. It is an opportunity to make a good first impression.

Answers

1 *What do you like about the place where you live?* asks for a personal opinion; *Where are you from?* asks for personal information.
2 *Where are you from?* can be answered with a short phrase; *What do you like about the place where you live?* needs a longer answer.

2 Ask students to briefly discuss this question in pairs first.

Suggested answer

Irene: she answers in sentences, not single words; she gives some extra details.

CD 1 Track 03

Examiner So, Irene, where are you from?

Irene: I'm from Llanes. It's a small town on the north coast of Spain, which becomes quite a busy tourist resort in the summer.

Examiner: And what do you like about Llanes?

Irene: Well, it's a fairly quiet place in the winter, so it has quite a relaxed atmosphere, but it's got wonderful beaches nearby and it's surrounded by lovely countryside. Also, I've got lots of friends in the area, so I have a very active social life. And of course, most of my family and relations live nearby, too.

Examiner: And you, Peter, where are you from?

Peter: Bremen, in northern Germany.

Examiner: And what do you like about Bremen?

Peter: My friends, the shops, the sports centre ...

Examiner: Do you come from a large family?

3 Tell students that the examiners are trained to recognise their ability to use appropriate vocabulary, including fixed phrases and collocations.

Extension idea Ask students to think of two or three other phrases with adjective(s) and a noun that they can add to the list. Round up ideas with the whole class and write appropriate phrases on the board for students to copy into their notebooks.

4 **Answers**

It is: a, c, d, e, f
It has: b, e, f, g, h, i, j, k, l

5 Pronunciation: word stress (1)

1 Tell students that pronunciation accounts for approximately 25% of the mark in the Speaking paper. The pronunciation syllabus in this course covers aspects of discourse including word stress, sentence stress, intonation, pausing and grouping, and linking. Pronunciation of phonemes is not covered, as difficulties in this area often result from interference from students' first language and vary depending on first language.

Answers

industrial, relaxed atmosphere, wonderful, important business, impressive, historic, attractive, residential

Extension idea 1 Ask students to read the complete phrases from the list in Exercise 3, concentrating on correct word stress.

Extension idea 2 To accustom students to using their dictionaries to check pronunciation, ask them to write four or five other words of two or more syllables on a piece of paper.

They should then check how each word is stressed in their dictionaries, but not mark the stress on their list.

They then exchange lists with a partner and, in pairs, take turns to read the words aloud. Students should correct and 'teach' their partners the correct stress for the words on their lists.

2 You can point out that students can check pronunciation and stress online in the Cambridge online dictionaries.

CD 1 Track 04

It's a large industrial city.

It has quite a relaxed atmosphere.

It has some wonderful beaches nearby.

It's an important business centre.

The city has some impressive architecture.

My town contains a lot of historic buildings.

Recently they have built several quite attractive buildings.

I live in a pleasant residential district of the city.

6 Tell students not to write out the sentences: they should rely on their ability to speak fluently without referring to notes.

7 Ask students to change partners for this exercise.

8 Tell students that this is not a discussion activity, i.e. they should actually take turns to answer the questions.

Alternative treatment Ask students to work in groups of three, with one student taking the role of examiner and asking the questions in turn to the other two students.

After three or four questions, they can change roles so that all students have practice at answering.

Writing | Part 1 An essay

As a warmer Ask students: *What is an essay? Do you ever have to write essays in (your own language)?* (An essay is a formal piece of academic writing where you discuss a question or an issue, outline information or research on the topic and argue your point of view, supporting it with reasons and examples.)

If so:

- *What sort of topics do you have to write about?*
- *How long are the essays?*
- *What things do you find difficult about writing an essay?*
- *What do you learn from writing essays?*

(Among points which might arise from the last question are: the need to research, think about the question, form an opinion, structure an answer and express the opinion convincingly the ability to support your opinion with reasons, facts and examples.)

If not:

- *What sort of writing do you have to do in your own language?*
- *How is it different from essay writing?*
- *What do you learn from doing formal writing as part of your school work?*

(Some of the answers may be the same as the points above.)

1 With books open, ask: *Why is it important to underline the points you must deal with?* (Answer: Because if you omit any points, or parts of your answer are irrelevant, you will lose marks.)

When students have finished, ask them to compare what they have underlined in pairs. Then round up with the whole class.

Suggested underlining
Teenagers and young people, share housework equally with their parents, agree, has more time, better, own idea

2 ***Extension idea*** When students have finished discussing, ask them to work alone and quickly note down the main points of their discussion alongside each of the points they underlined in the essay question.

Ask: *Do you have notes for all the points? If there is something you omitted in your discussion, what can you say about it?*

3 Also ask: *Does Violetta express any ideas which did not come up in your discussion?*

4 Ask students: *Why is it important to write a plan?* Tell them that they will get higher marks if their essay has a clear, logical organisation and structure and is divided clearly into paragraphs, each of which deals with a separate aspect of the subject.

Point out that the final paragraph of Violetta's essay is very short; the middle paragraphs, where she discusses the topic, are where most of the writing should take place.

Answers
Para. 1: e Para. 2: b Para. 3: c Para. 4: a
Para. 5: d

5 Ask students: *Why is it important to express your opinions in an essay?* (Answer: Because if you don't, you haven't answered the question or completed the task, which asks: *Do you agree?*)

Answers
I believe, In my view, in my opinion, I think

6 Tell students that it's important to be able to express a balanced opinion, i.e. to be able to express ideas that perhaps they don't agree with and then contrast them with the ideas they do agree with.

Ask them to look at how ideas are balanced and contrasted using these phrases.

Go through the Language reference on page 168 with students.

Answers
1 Although **2** However **3** On the other hand
4 However **5** whereas

7 **Answers**
1 whereas **2** Although **3** However / On the other hand **4** Although **5** On the other hand / However **6** However / On the other hand

Extension idea Ask students to write three sentences of their own using *although, however, on the other hand* and *whereas* to express contrasting ideas which came up during their discussion in Exercise 2.

8 Tell students that in the exam they will have approximately 40 minutes for this writing task. However, as this is the first writing task of the course, it is more important to do things well than to write to a time limit, and if they need to take a bit longer, they can.

Alternative treatment 1 Although this task is perhaps best done for homework, ask students to write a plan for the essay in class. Give them three or four minutes to do this.

When they are ready, ask them to compare their plans in pairs. Then round up with the whole class.

Alternative treatment 2 Ask students to read Violetta's answer again and underline any useful language which they could use in their own answers. Again, round up with the whole class.

Sample answer
See sample in Exercise 3 in the Student's Book.

Leisure and pleasure

Unit objectives

- **Reading and Use of English Part 5:** introduction to task type; training in skimming and answering multiple-choice questions
- **Reading and Use of English Part 4:** introduction to task type; writing key word transformations with comparative and superlative structures
- **Writing Part 2:** introduction to writing an article; structuring an article; paragraphing; writing compound and complex sentences; using adjectives
- **Listening Part 2:** introduction to task type; identifying/predicting the type of information required
- **Speaking Part 2:** introduction to task type; talking about free time and hobbies; giving a structured answer using discourse markers
- **Pronunciation**: sentence stress (1)
- **Vocabulary:** types of leisure-time activity; phrasal verbs and expressions, e.g. *take up, sum up, have a go,* etc.; adjectives describing feelings, e.g. *puzzled, motivating,* etc.
- **Grammar:** making comparisons; adjectives ending in *-ed* and *-ing*

Starting off

As a warmer Ask students to work in pairs and suggest names for each of the activities in the photographs. Encourage students to give reasons for their answers to question 2.

Suggested answers
(top left) playing football/soccer / a team sport; (top right) playing computer/video games; (middle) racing/riding a motorbike; (bottom left) parachuting/skydiving; (bottom middle) (window) shopping; (bottom right) exercising / going to the gym

Extension idea 1 Ask students to work in small groups. Tell them to list their leisure-time activities and compare them with the ones in the photographs using questions A–G.

Extension idea 2 If appropriate, ask students to bring photographs from home for the next class showing themselves or their families doing leisure activities, and ask them to talk about why they do the activities and how they feel about them.

Extension idea 3 On the board write:

- *In both photos …*
- *In the first photo… but in the second photo …*

Ask students to work in pairs and look at the top two photos. Ask them to think of (but not write) several sentences about the photos using the words given. (Suggested answers: In both photos, the young people are with their friends. In the first photo, they're playing a sport outside, but in the second photo, they're sitting inside at home.)

Round up ideas with the whole class and write some sentences as examples on the board.

Write: *Which is the most enjoyable?* on the board.

Ask students to work in pairs. They should each choose two other photos and take turns to compare the activities and say which they think is most enjoyable. (This may be treated as a simple introduction to Speaking Part 2, but at this stage, it's a good idea not to insist that they speak for a full minute or without interruption from their partner.)

Listening | Part 2

1 ***As a warmer*** With books closed, generate a class discussion by asking students:

- *Do you play video or computer games?*
- *Some people think that video games are a waste of time. Do you agree? Why? / Why not?*

Answers
1 encourage **2** distract **3** concentrate **4** develop **5** solve **6** require **7** make **8** contribute **9** waste

Extension idea 1 If your students did the warmer, ask them which of the ideas 1–9 came up in the discussion.

Extension idea 2 Tell students that some of the verbs in the exercise are followed by prepositions. Which ones? (Answers: *distract from; concentrate on; contribute to*)

Ask students to copy these into their notebooks and keep a section for verbs + dependent prepositions.

2 Ask students to work in pairs first, then have a class discussion.

3 Listening Part 2 tests students' understanding of details, specific information and opinions. While the incomplete sentences will be paraphrases of what they hear, they need to complete them by writing words exactly as they hear them in the recording.

Go through the Exam information box with students first. Tell them that they should make sure the completed sentences make sense. Although small spelling mistakes are permitted, they should try to spell their answers correctly.

Tell them that in the exam, they will have 45 seconds to read the questions and that they should use this time to identify the type of information they need to complete each sentence; this will help them to focus on what they need to listen for.

To get them started, elicit with the whole class that gap 1 may be something that you read.

Suggested answers
1 something you read **2** a job **3** something to do with games that he made with other students **4** a reason for working / something you can get from working **5** something which will help solve problems **6** something people have which is different to something he has **7** not something you do alone **8** something one of his games has become **9** something large games need **10** something he intends to start

4 ▶ After listening, ask students to work in pairs and read their completed sentences carefully to make sure they are grammatically accurate and spelled correctly.

Answers
1 science fiction **2** computer programmer **3** creation club **4** experience **5** experiments **6** skills and interests **7** social activity **8** film **9** several years **10** business (developing games)

CD 1 Track 05

Mike: Good morning. It's great to be visiting this school and talking to you. As you know, my name's Mike Selby and I'm a games developer. I thought I'd tell you a bit about my background and my job because for many young people, it's the sort of job they dream of doing – you know, turning your hobby into a career, so to speak. Well, it'll be no surprise to you that when I was a kid, I used to play video games and things like that. I was also a huge fan of [1]science fiction and I used to read whatever I could get my hands on. I spent hours doing that, even when my mum and dad thought I was up in my room doing my homework. Anyway, I never really expected to become a games developer. My aims when I was at school were a bit more realistic, I think, and my dream actually was to become a [2]computer programmer. I mean, I was good at developing software and I thought that'd be a much safer career where I'd make far more money than developing games. But you know, games were a bit of a passion of mine and while I was at school, I got together with a few of my friends and we set up something we called the 'games [3]creation club' – you know, we'd go through the process of having an idea, planning, sitting down and developing software and so on. At the time, it was just about the most exciting thing in my life, and I spent all my free time doing it. And then I was given this opportunity which was even better. Word got around that I was good at writing software, and a local company belonging to someone's dad offered me a summer job. Of course, I had planned to go travelling with friends, but the chance to gain [4]experience doing what I enjoyed was just too good to miss. In the end, I worked for the same people for two summers. I worked much harder than I ever worked at school and I loved every minute of it. Games development is the most creative thing you can imagine and you can go wherever your imagination takes you. I love it. I love working on the problems and I love carrying out [5]experiments to work out how to deal with those problems. Also, it's a very rich environment, and one thing which makes it so good is that I find myself working with colleagues whose [6]skills and interests are completely different from mine. I think that it actually helps to have a good diverse range of people in the team, and we all learn from each other. In fact, you probably have an image in your minds of a games developer sitting alone in front of a screen all day. In fact, it's an extremely [7]social activity – we're always swapping ideas, playing games together, even going out to the cinema as a group and picking up ideas there. While I'm on the subject, cinema is another of my passions, and one of the biggest thrills for me was when one of my games, *The Snake Quest*, was made into a [8]film. Have any of you seen it? You have? Great. I hope you liked it. Nowadays, I prefer to work on smaller games than that one, the reason being that those huge complex games take [9]several years to make, and I don't like to spend so much time on things. I prefer a bit more variety. Well, I hope I've managed to inspire a few of you here. Just to let you know that in the next few months, I'm planning to set up my own [10]business developing games and I'll certainly be looking out for new talent, so if any of you are interested, drop me a line – here's my email address – and I'd be pleased to hear from you. Thank you.

Extension idea Print out and photocopy the recording script from the Teacher's Resources CD-ROM. Ask students to check their answers with the recording script. You can play the recording again while they are doing this.

5 While students are discussing, monitor and note down any mistakes they make with comparisons of adjectives and adverbs which you can use as a warmer in the Grammar section which follows.

Extension idea Ask students to take turns to recommend a game to the whole class (or if the class is large, to their groups). To help them, write on the board:

- *What does the game involve?*
- *How long does it take?*
- *How difficult is it to play?*
- *Why will you enjoy playing it?*

Tell students to think about what they will say and make a few notes (they can do this in pairs if they wish). Meanwhile, help them with vocabulary where necessary.

When they have finished giving their talks, you can discuss with the whole class which games are most popular and most interesting to play.

Grammar

Making comparisons

1 ***As a warmer*** If you monitored and noted mistakes with comparisons of adjectives and adverbs while your students were doing Listening Exercise 5, either photocopy your notes or write salient mistakes on the board. Ask students to work in pairs or small groups and correct the mistakes.

After doing the exercise, go through the Language reference section on page 169 (Making comparisons) with students. As you go through it, ask them to suggest other examples for each 'rule'.

Answers
1 a bit more **2** much safer; far more **3** most **4** better **5** much harder **6** most **7** biggest **8** so much

2 Tell students it is important to look out for and avoid these mistakes when they are speaking and writing. If they notice that they have made a mistake, or they hear a classmate make a mistake, they should correct it.

Answers
1 ~~the healthier~~ the healthiest **2** ~~more cheaper~~ cheaper **3** ~~that~~ than **4** ~~more hardly~~ harder **5** ~~as often than~~ as often as **6** ~~the more risky~~ the riskiest / the most risky **7** ~~the less interesting~~ the least interesting **8** ~~more good~~ better

Extension idea Students work in pairs. Ask them to say which sentences they agree with and which they disagree with, and why.

3 To get students started, elicit a sentence for the first question from the class and write it on the board.

When students have completed all the sentences, ask them to compare their ideas in pairs or small groups.

Suggested answers
1 difficult to park in the city. **2** difficult as it looks. **3** important thing is to participate, not to win. **4** skiing than skating. **5** nicer than I am. **6** as bad for you as some people say.

Extension idea Ask students to discuss which of their partner's sentences they agree/disagree with and why.

Note: This may be a suitable moment to do the photocopiable activity on the Teacher's Resources CD-ROM.

Reading and Use of English | Part 5

1 ***As a warmer*** Ask students to look at the photo of Ewan McGregor and say what they know about him (he has starred in many films including *Trainspotting, Star Wars, Down with Love, Cassandra's Dream, Moulin Rouge* and *Amelia*).

Ask how many of your class ride motorbikes and how their families feel about them riding motorbikes. (This is a question you can also perhaps ask to students who don't ride motorbikes.)

2 Reading and Use of English Part 5 tests students' understanding of main ideas, details, attitudes and opinions. They may also have to deduce the meaning of a word or phrase and to grasp implication from clues in the text. Tell them that it is important to skim the text before reading it more methodically to deal with the multiple-choice questions which follow.

Skimming is reading quickly or superficially to get a general idea of the content and structure of a passage without trying to understand it in detail or deal with difficult vocabulary or concepts. Tell students that by skimming, they will be able to locate the answers more quickly when they come to the multiple-choice questions. Give them a time limit of three minutes. When they have finished, ask them to work in pairs and summarise the reasons in their own words.

Suggested answers
His girlfriend left him for someone with a motorbike; he had enjoyed riding a motorbike when he was six; it would allow him to get to places.

3 and 4 Tell students that the best way to deal with multiple-choice questions is to:

- underline the key idea in the question, but not at this stage read the options A–D
- locate where the question is dealt with in the text and read that section carefully, underlining the words which answer the question
- then look at the options and choose the answer which corresponds with the words they have underlined.

Suggested underlining
1 Such trivialities **2** did not buy **3** adults, frightened, because **4** main reason for buying **5** desire, meant **6** result, accident

Point out that the answers occur in the text in the same order as the questions, so students should work through the questions and the text in the same order.

Ask them to work alone and then to compare their answers in pairs before rounding up with the whole class.

Answers
1 D **2** B **3** C **4** D **5** A **6** C

Extension idea Ask students: *What impression do you have of Ewan McGregor as a teenager? Was he a typical teenager? In what ways?*

5 ***As a warmer*** Ask students to brainstorm reasons why teenagers often want a motorbike; ask them to brainstorm reasons why parents often don't want their children to have motorbikes.

Before they do the role play, ask them to work in pairs and give them two or three minutes to prepare roles for either Student A or Student B. Then ask them to change partners and work with someone who prepared the other role.

Vocabulary

Phrasal verbs and expressions

1 EP Tell students that in Reading and Use of English Part 5, they must be able to guess the meanings of words and phrases from the context. Ask students to:

- find the phrasal verbs and expressions in the reading text before choosing the answers
- copy the verbs and expressions into their notebooks.

Alternative treatment Ask students not to look at the definitions in the right-hand column. They should work in pairs and discuss what each phrasal verb or expression might mean by looking at the context.

To get them started you can elicit clues which will help them to guess the meaning of *take up*: *first* and *biking beginnings* should bring them close to the meaning.

Answers
1 d **2** a **3** h **4** f **5** g **6** c **7** b **8** e

2 **Answers**
1 taking risks **2** sum up **3** have a go **4** make up **5** didn't have / hadn't got a clue **6** keep a promise / keep promises **7** taking up **8** get hold of

Extension idea Students work in pairs and write four sentences using phrasal verbs and expressions from this section, but leaving a gap where the phrasal verbs should be. They then test another pair by giving them their sentences and asking them to write the phrasal verb in the correct form in the gap.

Grammar

Adjectives with *-ed* and *-ing*

1 After doing this introductory exercise, go through the Language reference section on page 163 (Adjectives with *-ed* and *-ing*) with the class.

Answers
1 thrilled, elated **2** exciting

Extension idea Ask students to brainstorm other adjectives they know with *-ed* and *-ing*.

2 Tell students that they should look out for and avoid these mistakes when they are speaking or writing. Tell them they can also correct their classmates if they hear them making a mistake.

Answers
1 amusing **2** irritating **3** bored **4** confused **5** embarrassing **6** excited

3 EP This exercise practises similar skills to those needed for Reading and Use of English Part 3 (word formation), where forming adjectives with *-ed* or *-ing* may be tested. However, in the exam, a continuous text is used rather than separate sentences.

Make sure that students spell their answers correctly. They may have difficulty with the 'y' in *worry*. Check also that they drop the final 'e' of *amuse* when writing *amusing*. If you wish, go through relevant parts of the section on spelling in the Language reference section on page 176.

Answers
1 astonishing **2** puzzled **3** motivating **4** worried **5** amusing **6** exhausted

4 Ask students to listen to the general gist of the story, as the recording contains a number of distractors.

Answer
g

CD 1 Track 06

Young woman: The whole experience was [1]amazing actually. I mean, I'd been working really hard, studying, and so I was feeling pretty [2]tired and nervous already, so when my boyfriend suggested I went along with him, I was like, [3]shocked, like 'No way!' – I mean the thought of breaking a bone or something even worse just before an exam was [4]terrifying. But you know, he just kept on at me, so for the sake of a bit of peace, in the end I said yes. When we were up there in the sky, I was just so [5]scared I can't tell you. I just wanted to get out of the plane. I felt trapped, but the only way to do that was to jump, and in fact, the jump itself was really [6]thrilling. I'd love to do it again. And I didn't break a thing!

5 ***Alternative treatment*** Before playing the recording again, ask students to work in pairs or small groups and try to remember what adjectives the girl used for each of these things. Students then listen again to check their answers.

Answers
2 tired and nervous **3** shocked **4** terrifying **5** scared and trapped **6** thrilling

6 Encourage students to use adjectives with *-ed* and *-ing*. If any students have problems, tell them they can talk about someone they know or give a fictional answer.

Reading and Use of English | Part 4

Reading and Use of English Part 4 tests students' knowledge of grammar, lexis and structure and their ability to express meaning using different structures.

Since this is students' first encounter with a complex exam task, go through the Exam information box with them and tell them:

- to concentrate on achieving the same meaning
- that although the sentences here practise comparison of adjectives and adverbs, questions in the exam may test a wide range of grammar, vocabulary and structures.

Go through the example (0). Point out that the answer:

- has between two and five words
- uses the key word in capitals without changing it in any way
- means the same as the original sentence.

Elicit answers to the first question from the whole class and write them on the board. Ask students to check the same criteria (between two and five words, key word unchanged, same meaning) and, if students suggest more than one answer, ask them to decide which answer is correct.

Ask them to do the rest of the exercise in pairs. Tell them to use the Language reference section on page 169 to help them.

Alternative treatment Write these 'answers' to question 1 on the board and ask students why they are wrong:

- *one instrument which is easier than all other* (too many words; does not mean the same)
- *easier than most other* (does not use the key word)
- *one of the more difficult* (does not mean the same).

Answers
1 one of the easiest **2** not as/so interesting as **3** play tennis so/as well as **4** is the noisiest person in **5** not as/so cheap as **6** more quickly than

Speaking | Part 2

1 Speaking Part 2 tests students' ability to organise their ideas and express themselves coherently and at length using suitable language.

As a warmer With books closed, ask students: *Do you think young people in your/this country spend too much time studying? What, for you, are the best ways of relaxing in your free time?*

With books open, go through the Exam information box with them.

Tell students that the photos are a starting point for them to speak.

In the exam, candidates will take it in turns to speak for one minute about a different pair of photographs. The candidate who is not speaking will be asked a question at the end about their partner's photographs.

Tell students they should compare the photos fairly generally, focusing on the main idea or subject of the photo, not the small details; they should move on to use the photos to answer the printed question.

At this stage, tell students they are not actually doing the task, but thinking of ideas.

2 ▶ Students can answer the question in pairs.

Suggested answers
Football: getting exercise, good for you, good for health, helps you relax, having fun, laughing, builds up social relationships and friendships, breaks down social boundaries between boys and girls **Chatting in a café:** communicating, sharing ideas and experiences, talk about problems, relax, enjoy friendship

Extension idea Ask students: *Which of the ideas Martyna expresses did you also think of?*

CD 1 Track 07

Examiner: In this part of the test, I'm going to give each of you two photographs. I'd like you to talk about your photographs on your own for about a minute, and also to answer a short question about your partner's photographs. Martyna, it's your turn first. Here are your photographs. They show people doing different activities in their free time. I'd like you to compare the photographs, and say how you think the people can benefit from spending their free time doing these different activities. All right?

Martyna: Well, in the first photo, there's a group of children, both boys and girls, playing football together in the park. They don't seem to be taking the game too seriously and they seem to be enjoying themselves. I think they benefit from this in several ways. Firstly, they're getting some exercise, which is always good for you because it's great for your health and helps you to relax. At the same time, they're having fun together, which is important because it builds up their social relationships and their friendships. Also, it's good to see boys and girls doing a bit of sport together instead of separately, because I think it helps break down social boundaries between boys and girls.

In the second photo, there are four girls chatting together in a café and laughing. They aren't so active as the children in the first photo because they're not doing a sport, but they are probably communicating more and sharing their ideas and experiences. I think they also benefit because they can talk about their problems, relax and also enjoy their friendship. Mm, all in all, I think they get a lot fr–

Examiner: Thank you.

Martyna: –om both activities.

3 ***Alternative treatment*** Before students listen again, ask them in pairs to discuss which of the points on the checklist are good things to do in the exam, which are not so good, and which are neither good nor bad.

Suggested answers
1 neither good nor bad **2** not so good – candidates are expected to make a broad general comparison **3** neither good nor bad – candidates can deal with each in turn or both at the same time **4** good – the photos are intended to lead to the question **5** good – this is clearly comparing **6** not so good – answers should be relevant **7** good

Answers
✓ 3, 4, 5, 7

4 Tell students not to write their answers and that they needn't remember Martyna's exact words.

Ask them:

- Which words/phrases introduce an answer to the question? (Answers: *I think they benefit; I think they also benefit because*)
- Which words/phrases introduce extra ideas and help Martyna to structure her answer? (Answers: *Firstly, At the same time, Also*)
- Which phrase introduces a short conclusion? (Answer: *all in all*)

Answers
See recording script for Track 7.

5 **Answers**
a 1 **b** 2 **c** 3, 4, 5

6 **Answers**
b First of all, To start with
c Besides, In addition, What is more

7 **Pronunciation:** sentence stress (1)

Remind students that stressing particular words in a sentence involves taking longer to say them and saying them more clearly. Good sentence stress is essential to clear communication.

1 ▶ Point out that it is the speaker who chooses which words to stress, i.e. there aren't words which must be stressed, but that it depends on what the speaker wants to communicate. Therefore, if students choose different words from the ones Martyna in fact stresses, this does not indicate wrong pronunciation.

CD 1 Track 08

1 Firstly, they're getting some exercise, which is always good for you.
2 It's great for your health and helps you to relax.
3 At the same time, they're having fun together …
4 … which is important because it builds up their social relationships and their friendships.
5 Also, it's good to see boys and girls doing a bit of sport together instead of separately.
6 I think it helps break down social boundaries between boys and girls.

2 ***Alternative treatment*** Ask students to take turns to read the sentences, but the student who is listening should chime in and say the stressed word at the same time as the student who is reading, e.g.
Student 1: Firstly, they're getting some exercise, which is always good for you.

Student 2: Firstly .... exercise .... good ....

3 ***Alternative treatment*** Ask students to do the same alternative treatment as for Pronunciation Exercise 2.

8 While students are doing the exercise, be strict with timing: look at your watch when you tell them to start and say 'Thank you' at the end of the minute. You can tell students that in the exam, the examiner will be strict with the timing to give all candidates exactly the same opportunity to speak and that an interruption from the examiner is not an indication of their performance.

Give students time to feed back to their partners. When they have finished, round up with the whole class and discuss any issues arising.

Extension idea Tell the student who is not speaking not to interrupt and to listen carefully. At the end, ask them one of these two questions:

- *Which activity would you prefer to do?*
- *Which of the activities do you think would be easiest to do?*

9 Tell students that this is an opportunity to put the feedback they have given into practice themselves.

Tell them to follow the same procedure as for Exercise 8.

Extension idea You can use the same extension idea as in Exercise 8.

Writing | Part 2 An article

1 ***As a warmer*** Ask students: *Have you ever written an article? What was it about? Where was it published? Do you enjoy reading articles written by other students, for example in college magazines? Why? / Why not? What sort of articles are most enjoyable?*

Point out that it is important to identify who is going to read the article – this will determine what they put in the article and the style they will use.

Suggested underlining
magazine for teenagers, leisure-time activity, How did you get started?, Why do you enjoy it so much?

2 Encourage students to speak for at least a minute.

3 ***Alternative treatment*** Ask students to read the article quite quickly without looking at the instructions for this exercise. Ask them: *What is wrong with the article?* (Answer: It's not divided into paragraphs.) *What effect does this have on the reader?* (Answer: It becomes difficult to follow the argument because it is not clearly structured.)

Point out that some paragraphs, especially introductory or concluding paragraphs, can be quite short and may sometimes have just one sentence. However, it is equally confusing when every paragraph is just one sentence long.

Answers and suggested answers
1 Para. 1: I first got interested … simple dishes at first; Para. 2: I found I really enjoyed cooking … usually ate the food quite happily; Para. 3: When I went back to school … enjoying a meal I've cooked; Para. 4: I'd recommend … that anyone can do.
2 Para. 1: how I started; Para. 2: how I continued; Para. 3: why I enjoy it; Para. 4: why I'd recommend it

4 **Suggested answers**
1 I found I really enjoyed cooking; I was soon doing things which were more complicated.
2 My younger brother and sister complained about some of my dishes; they usually ate the food quite happily.
3 When friends come round to my house I often cook them something; I find it really satisfying and relaxing.
4 I'd recommend it as a hobby; for me, it's one of the most creative and useful free-time activities that anyone can do.
5 When I went back to school after the summer, I decided to do cookery lessons; now I think I'm quite a competent cook.

5 **Suggested answers**
2 I got interested in flying when I was about 14 because my father took me to an airshow.
3 My parents don't want me to fly because they think it is dangerous.
4 One of my friends is learning to fly and he's asked me to come with him because he thinks I'd like it.

6 **Suggested answers**
2 I was staying with my aunt. My aunt is a keen cook.
3 I was soon doing things. They / The things were more complicated.
4 I went back to school after the summer. I decided to do cookery lessons.
5 Friends come round to my house. I often cook my friends / them something.
6 For me, cooking is one of the most creative and useful free-time activities. Anyone can cook / do it.

7 **Suggested answers**
1 I was 13 when I started running seriously / I started running seriously when I was 13.
2 My aunt, who is a keen athlete, encouraged me.
3 I go running most days when/after I've finished school and done my homework.
4 Running is a sport which/that gets you really fit.

8 **Suggested answers**
1 I started windsurfing when I was 13 and I was staying with friends by the sea.
2 One of my friends, who is a keen windsurfer, encouraged me to start because she thought I would enjoy it.
3 I kept falling into the sea to start with because it was a fairly windy day and there were a lot of waves.
4 I didn't enjoy it at first because I had to concentrate quite hard, but I carried on trying.
5 I started to windsurf quite fast, which was exciting, so I started to find it quite enjoyable.

9 Remind students that they will get marks for the range and appropriateness of their vocabulary.

Answers
1 satisfying, relaxing, fascinating, wonderful
2 creative, useful **3** competent

10 ***Alternative treatment*** Print out and photocopy the word list for this unit from the Teacher's Resources CD-ROM. Ask students to refer to it while doing this exercise.

Answers

feelings about an activity	the type of activity
astonishing, delightful, depressing, dreadful, entertaining, exhausting, incredible, irritating, superb, tremendous, unbelievable	competitive, demanding, economical, popular, time-consuming

Extension idea Ask students to choose three words which are new to them. Ask them to write a sentence using each of them.

They should then compare their ideas with examples from a learner's dictionary.

Divide students into three teams and ask them to take turns to read sentences they have written to the whole class, who then discuss if the word has been used correctly or not. You should act as referee. If the word has been used correctly, the team scores a point.

The winning team is the one which scores the most points.

11 ***Extension idea*** Ask students:

- *What are the characteristics of a good article?* (Possible answers: It must be interesting, tell the reader something they didn't know, be enjoyable to read.)
- *What would be a suitable style for this article? Why?* (Answer: As it's for a magazine for teenagers, a neutral or informal style would be suitable.)

Remind students to use some compound sentences.

12 If you wish, this task can be done for homework.

- For more on writing articles, you can refer students to page 193 (Writing reference – Articles).

Sample answer
See the model in Exercise 3 in the Student's Book.

Extension idea Collect students' articles, photocopy them and staple them to form a class magazine.

Vocabulary and grammar review Unit 1

1 **2** bad-tempered **3** hardworking/hard-working **4** unreliable **5** anxious **6** sensitive **7** mature **8** concerned/anxious

2 **1** clear; up **2** pick; up **3** get on with **4** worn; out **5** do up **6** went on

3 **1** do **2** make **3** do **4** doing **5** do **6** made **7** made **8** making

4 **1** won **2** have arrived; have been expecting **3** have spent; has turned up **4** have been having / have had; has been telling / has told; has not told; has seen **5** has lost / has been losing; has been getting **6** has finished; have been waiting **7** has eaten; has not left **8** has been looking; has been studying

Vocabulary and grammar review Unit 2

1 **1** keep a promise / promises **2** to take / taking risks **3** taking up **4** make up **5** sum up **6** haven't / haven't got / don't have a clue; have a go

2 **Suggested answers**

1. Katya took up karate when she was seven years old because she was interested in it.
2. Her father, who is a professional karate instructor, taught her, so she progressed quickly and soon became junior regional champion.
3. She did karate with other children who were the same age as her, but none of them was as good as her, so she felt dissatisfied.
4. Last year, she participated in the national championship, but she did not win because she was injured during one of the matches.
5. She hopes to become a professional karate instructor and work in the same sports centre as her father because he has too many students.
6. Some of her father's students have been studying karate for several years, and her father thinks they would benefit from a different teacher because they are too familiar with his style of karate.

3 **1** motorbike made more noise than **2** are not as/so dangerous **3** is the best player **4** as/so stressed as **5** much more clearly than **6** more comfortable than any of

4 **1** amazing **2** exhausting **3** puzzling **4** disappointed **5** motivated **6** astonished

3 Happy holidays?

Unit objectives

- **Reading and Use of English Part 3:** introduction to task type; word formation: forming adjectives from verbs and nouns
- **Reading and Use of English Part 7:** introduction to task type; studying the questions before the text; locating information
- **Writing Part 2:** introduction to writing a report; brainstorming ideas; using a range of tenses; format and structure of a report
- **Listening Part 3:** introduction to task type
- **Speaking Part 3:** introduction to task type; dealing with all the prompts; making suggestions and asking opinions; agreeing and disagreeing; strategies for discussing and deciding which option(s) to choose; phrases to involve partners in discussion
- **Pronunciation:** intonation
- **Vocabulary:** lexis connected with travel and holidays; confusion between *travel, journey, trip* and *way*; adjective collocations with *journey* and *trip*; phrases to talk about travel; adjective suffixes
- **Grammar:** past simple, past continuous and *used to*; spelling when adding *-ed* to past tense verbs; *at, in* or *on* in time phrases; past perfect simple and continuous

Starting off

1 ***Alternative treatment*** Before doing the task, students work in small groups and:

- cover the text in their books and look at the photographs only
- brainstorm vocabulary they could use to talk about each of the photographs, e.g. for photo 1, *camping, at a campsite,* etc.
- then check their ideas against the vocabulary in the box before doing the task in the book.

Answers

types of holiday	holiday locations and places to stay	holiday activities
a camping holiday	at a campsite	walking and climbing
a beach holiday	at a luxury hotel	meeting new people
a sightseeing tour	on a cruise ship	sunbathing
a cruise	at a youth hostel	relaxing
backpacking	in the city centre	visiting monuments
	at the seaside	seeing new places

Extension idea If students did the alternative treatment above, ask them to add any extra words/phrases they thought of to the table.

2 ***Extension idea*** Ask students to work in pairs and suggest and describe two more photographs which could be added to the set.

Suggested answers

1 Photo 1: a camping holiday
Photo 2: a sightseeing holiday
Photo 3: backpacking
Photo 4: a beach holiday
Photo 5: a cruise

2 On camping holidays, people walk, climb, relax and see new places;on sightseeing holidays, they see new places and visit monuments; when backpacking, they meet new people, walk, go sightseeing and see new places; on beach holidays, people relax and sunbathe; on a cruise, they meet new people, see new places, visit monuments, sunbathe and relax.

Listening | Part 3

1 Listening Part 3 tests students' ability to understand gist, detail, purpose, opinion, situation, etc. from five short extracts.

Before doing the exercise, go through the Exam information box with students. Tell them that in the exam, they will have 30 seconds to look at the questions and that they should use this time to underline the key ideas; this will help them to focus on what they need to listen for.

Suggested underlining
B didn't mind, discomfort **C** know, people **D** similar before **E** low-cost holiday **F** didn't do much during the day **G** (not) in as much danger as, imagined **H** a break from my parents

Extension idea Tell students that

they will not hear the answers expressed using exactly the same words as in the question. To sensitise them to this point, carry out the procedure below, but tell them they won't have time to do this in the exam itself.

Ask them to work in pairs and paraphrase each statement using their own words to predict how the statements might be expressed in the recording.

When they have finished, elicit suggestions for each question from the whole class.

As a follow-up, do the extension idea in Exercise 2 after you have done Exercise 2.

2 

Answers
1 G **2** F **3** D **4** A **5** C

Extension idea When students have listened twice, ask them to compare their answers in pairs.

Ask them to remember, approximately, the words each speaker said which gave them the answers and to compare these with the ideas they, the students, had when doing the extension idea in Exercise 1.

Follow up by printing out and photocopying the recording script from the Teacher's Resources CD-ROM. Ask students to underline the words which gave them the answers (see the recording script for Track 9).

CD 1 Track 09

Presenter: One. Francesca.

Francesca: I went on one of those journeys overland to Kenya. It was awesome to be able to go off with a group of people my own age. I mean, really, on family holidays we always used to go to the same campsite and lie on the same beach and things. This was a whole new thing – seeing completely different places and doing lots of things I'd never done before. We did have a driver and a guide to keep an eye on things, so [1]<u>I don't think there was anything particularly risky about it, even though my mum and gran worried</u> from the moment I left to the moment I got back!

Presenter: Two. Mike.

Mike: It was the nightlife we went for really. I went with a couple of my mates, you know, [2]<u>we got up late in the morning or even in the afternoon and usually hung around by the pool till sunset chilling out</u> or we made a trip to the beach, which was only about 20 minutes away by bus. Except of course on days when it was cloudy. But at night, we were down at the clubs, partying to the small hours, getting back to the hotel at two or three in the morning. And surprise, surprise, we managed to get through all our cash!

Presenter: Three. Sally.

Sally: I went off with a couple of my friends in March. We were out in the open air in these amazing mountain landscapes and doing some awesome climbing. We all complained about what we cooked, though, and the weather caused a few problems. We were on our way back down the mountain when we got caught in this really big storm, so that was a bit scary. [3]<u>But I'd done that sort of thing quite a lot with my dad when I was a kid</u> – um, my dad used to be a climber when he was younger – so I knew what I was doing.

Presenter: Four. Paul.

Paul: Well, [4]<u>it wasn't really my idea of a good time at all</u>. The meals were good, if you don't mind sitting around with a lot of middle-aged adults in smart hotels. It was just really dull. And Mum and Dad dragged me round looking at paintings and sculptures, which was just so boring! [4]<u>Still, there was an upside</u>, because while we were going round yet another museum, I got to meet this Polish girl called Jolanta. She was about as fed up as I was, so we just dumped our parents and went off for the day together. [4]<u>We had a really great time</u> and, actually, we're still in touch.

Presenter: Five. Katie.

Katie: It was one of my first non-family holidays too, except for a couple of summer camps when I was younger. I went backpacking with some mates round Europe, using the trains mainly, and we stayed in youth hostels, which saved us a bit of money. [5]<u>There were hundreds of other people like us from all over the world who were doing the same sort of thing</u>. It was good fun, a great atmosphere. I really like that sort of mixing of cultures – it's one of the best things about foreign travel, so I'm hoping we'll do it again next year.

3 If your students have not had holidays with friends, you can ask them: *How does your family decide what sort of holiday to have? What do different members of your family particularly enjoy doing on holiday?*

Extension idea Round up opinions by asking the class to vote on which they prefer: holidays with family, or holidays with friends.

Grammar

Past simple, past continuous and *used to*

1 **When** students have done the exercise, go through the explanation in the Language reference section on page 179 with them (Past simple, past continuous and *used to*).

Alternative treatment If students have access to the

recording script, ask them to check their answers using this, instead of listening again.

Answers
1 used to go **2** used to be **3** was **4** were going **5** got **6** dumped **7** went **8** had **9** stayed **10** were doing

2 Encourage students to refer to the Language reference section on page 179 while they do this exercise.

Answers
1 was walking **2** used to do **3** got; jumped; rode **4** used to spend **5** were walking; began **6** used to visit; was

3 When students have completed the exercise, ask them to check their answers by referring to the Language reference section on page 179.

Answers
developed, enjoyed, happened, mentioned, occurred, opened, planned, preferred, stopped, studied, travelled (BrE) / traveled (AmE), tried

Extension idea Ask students to write their own example verbs + *-ed* for each of the 'rules' in the Language reference section.

Vocabulary

travel, journey, trip and *way*

1 If your students all speak the same language, you can ask them how they would translate each of the words into their language.

Answers
1 trip **2** Way **3** travel **4** journey

Extension idea Ask students to write their own examples to show the differences in meaning.

2 Tell students that they should pay special attention when using these words, as candidates often make mistakes with them in the exam.

Answers
1 trip **2** way **3** trip **4** trip **5** travel **6** journey **7** trip **8** journey **9** way

3 Ask students to underline any words in the list for which they are unsure of the meaning. They should then discuss in pairs what each of the words they have underlined means.

Print out and photocopy the word list for this unit from the Teacher's Resources CD-ROM, so students can check their ideas.

Alternative treatment Ask students to cover the list while they do the exercise. When they have finished, they can uncover it to check their answers.

Answers
1 pleasant/safe/successful **2** overnight **3** outward **4** shopping **5** forthcoming **6** safe/pleasant

Extension idea Ask students to write three more sentences using other collocations from the list.

4 ***Alternative treatment*** Do the photocopiable activity on the Teacher's Resources CD-ROM, which is quite similar.

Reading and Use of English | Part 3

EP Reading and Use of English Part 3 tests students' ability to form words by adding affixes and, in some cases, compounds to fit the context of a short text. They may also need to make internal changes to some words (e.g. *high – height*). Students therefore need to understand the text and recognise what part of speech is required for each gap, whether it has an affirmative or negative meaning, is singular or plural, etc.

The best general preparation students can have for this exam task is to read extensively to build up their vocabulary.

1 ***As a warmer*** EP To sensitise students to some of the changes that may be needed, with books closed, write these adjectives on the board: *critical, industrial, innocent, unhelpful, unbelievable, artistic.*

Ask students:

- *What type of word are all of these?* (Answer: adjectives)
- *In pairs, write a noun or verb for each of these adjectives.* (Answers: *critic* (noun) / *criticise* (verb); *industry; innocence; help; believe; art/artist*)

When students have finished, round up and check spelling.

Ask:

- *What ways of forming adjectives can you see here?* (Answers: adding *-al, -ful, -able, -ic* and changing *-ence* to *-ent*)
- *Can you think of any other ways of forming adjectives?*

You can point out that there are a number of ways of changing nouns and verbs into adjectives, but there is no general rule to say which way should be used when.

With books open, draw students' attention to spelling changes which occur, e.g. dropping the final 'e' in *nature – natural*; 'y' becomes 'i' as in *mystery – mysterious*.

Tell students that for this task, the word must be spelled correctly. If you wish, refer them to the spelling section in the Language reference on page 176.

Answers
2 adventurous **3** friendly **4** memorable **5** mysterious **6** risky **7** crowded **8** thrilled/ thrilling **9** doubtful **10** successful **11** remarkable **12** accessible

Extension idea Ask students to suggest other adjectives formed in the same ways.

2 EP In some cases, there is more than one correct answer. Encourage students to think of as many possibilities as they can. They will also suggest negative adjectives, so it is worth pointing out that these can sometimes be formed with the suffix *-less*. You can elicit other ways of making them negative (they have seen some in Unit 1), e.g. adding prefixes: *dis-*, *ir-*, *im-*, *in-* and *un-*.

Alternative treatment Print out and photocopy the word list for this unit from the Teacher's Resources CD-ROM and ask students to check their answers, including spelling, and the meaning of each word.

Answers
artist – artistic; caution – cautious; colour – colourful, colourless; educate – educational, educated; emotion – emotional; energy – energetic; mass – massive; predict – predictable; reason – reasonable; respond – responsible; storm – stormy; thought – thoughtful, thoughtless; wealth – wealthy

Extension idea Students can use English–English dictionaries to explore the differences in meaning between adjectives formed from the same base word, e.g. *thoughtful, thoughtless*. Ask them also to write their own examples.

3 EP Tell students it is important to understand the text and to identify what type of word (noun/verb/ adjective/adverb) is missing, whether it has an affirmative or negative meaning, etc. in order to answer the questions, so they should read the title and the text fairly quickly before they start to get a general idea of what it is about. In the exam, any type of word is possible – noun, verb, adverb, adjective – but here only adjectives are worked on.

Answers
1 uncomfortable **2** thoughtful **3** colourful **4** unforgettable **5** optimistic **6** considerable **7** anxious **8** sympathetic

4 Get students started by eliciting one or two ideas, e.g. missing your flight or your train; not having the right ticket, etc.

Ask students: *Have any of these things ever happened to you? Tell each other about it.*

Grammar

at, *in* or *on* in time phrases

1 **Answers**
1 in, in **2** on **3** at, at **4** in

Extension idea Before looking at the Language reference, ask students in small groups to think of simple 'rules' for when to use *at*, *in* and *on* in time phrases based on these sentences, e.g. *in* + parts of days. When they have finished, round up with the class, then ask them to check their 'rules' with the Language reference on page 172.

2 Tell students they should pay special attention when using these prepositions in time phrases, as candidates frequently make mistakes.

Answers
1 ~~on July~~ in July **2** ~~In the weekends~~ At the weekends*… ~~on the afternoon~~ in the afternoon **3** ~~in 11.00~~ at 11.00 **4** correct **5** ~~at 2008~~ in 2008 **6** correct **7** ~~in certain times~~ at certain times **8** ~~at the morning in a normal day~~ in the morning on a normal day
*Note: *on the weekends* is correct in American English.

Extension idea Tell students to note down on a piece of paper two things they do regularly and two things they did, or which happened to them last year, but they shouldn't note down when they do/did these things, e.g. *I play football. I visited London.*

They then work in pairs and take turns to ask *yes/no* questions to find out when their partners do/did the things they noted down, e.g. *'Do you play football at weekends?' 'Yes.' 'Do you play on Saturday mornings?' 'No.' 'Do you play on Saturday afternoons?' 'Yes.'*

Reading and Use of English | Part 7

1 ***As a warmer*** Tell students they are going to read about holidays which went wrong. Tell them not to read yet, but to just look at the photos accompanying each section on page 35. In pairs or small groups, ask them:

- *Where do you think each photo was taken?*
- *What do you think might have gone wrong with each holiday?*

Before doing the exercise, go through the Exam information box with students.

Alternative treatment To encourage brainstorming, ask students to think of at least eight things which can spoil people's holidays, e.g. the weather, and note them down. Tell them that it is a race and the group which completes a list of eight things first is the winner.

When they have finished, ask groups to think of examples for each of the things they have noted down.

Finally, ask groups to present their ideas to the rest of the class.

2 Reading and Use of English Part 7 tests students' ability to locate which section of text contains details, opinions and attitudes expressed in the questions. Students need to be able to distinguish the correct section from other sections which may contain information or opinions which appear similar.

Point out to students that in this reading task, the questions are printed before the text; they should therefore take time to familiarise themselves with the questions before they approach the text. If they do this, they will know what information they have to find and will recognise it more quickly when they start reading.

Tell them that if they are familiar with the ten questions, they may only need to read each section once to find the answers.

Suggested underlining
1 hide from danger **2** employee intimidating **3** not pleased, spend so long **4** visited, previous occasion **5** worried, strong **6** missed speaking, people **7** painful experience **8** travelled with, ex-criminal **9** unaware, danger **10** holiday, mistake, before arriving

Extension idea When students have finished underlining, ask them to work in small groups, and with books closed, see how many of the questions they can remember.

3 Tell students it is important to find evidence in the text for their choices, so they should underline words/phrases/sentences which support their choices.

Alternative treatment To make this a communicative activity, you can follow this procedure:

- Ask students to work in pairs. Tell each pair to read either sections A and C or sections B and D. Tell them to find the questions which correspond to their sections.
- Give them seven minutes for this.
- They then work with another pair and explain which questions correspond to their extract and why (they should quote the words in the extract which support their answers).
- Tell them to discuss any problems, e.g. two students have chosen the same question, or there is a question that no one has found an extract for.

This activity will help students to read all the questions carefully and find evidence in the text to support their answers.

Answers
1 B **2** C **3** C **4** D **5** B **6** D **7** A **8** C **9** A **10** D

4 To help students talk about memorable holidays, you can write these questions on the board:

- *When did you have the holiday?*
- *Who were you with?*
- *What happened?*
- *How did you feel?*

Ask students to think and plan for a minute or two before speaking.

Grammar

Past perfect simple and continuous

1 When you have finished these questions, go through the explanation for the past perfect simple in the Language reference section on page 179 (Past perfect simple and continuous) with your students.

Answers
1 A
2 had organised (past perfect)
3 In the first sentence, her father organised the trip before they arrived; in the second sentence, he organised it when they were already in the country.

2 ***Alternative treatment*** To encourage scanning skills, give students two minutes to locate six examples.

Answers
A Pauline Vernon: *until that point, no one* ***had bothered*** *to mention the sea-snakes – The sting, on both legs, was agony, …*
B Sandy Henderson: *we****'d passed*** *a small cabin a little way back on the trail – we made a dash for that*
C Cat O'Donovan: *what I* ***had let*** *myself in for – Twenty-three hours into an epic bus trip across the States, I began to wonder; I* ***had been filled*** *with romantic ideas – Before boarding the first bus in LA; After the guy next to me* ***had finished*** *talking about his time in jail – I realised my expectations were a bit off; she* ***had eaten*** *several passengers – One unfriendly staff member was so large I feared*

3 You can elicit why in question 3, both *organised* and *had organised* are correct (Answer: Because the use of *before* makes the time frame clear).

Answers
1 had eaten **2** had never been **3** organised / had organised **4** arrived; had lost **5** recognised; had never spoken **6** had damaged

4 After answering this question, go through the explanation for the past perfect continuous in the Language reference section on page 179.

Answers
1 A
2 A past perfect continuous, B past perfect simple

5 **Answers**
1 had been living **2** had been walking; began **3** had already finished; offered **4** had only been speaking **5** got; had been walking

6 Tell students to take extra care when using past tenses, as mistakes can lead to confusion.

Answers
1 ~~have done~~ had done **2** ~~didn't have~~ hadn't had **3** ~~didn't go~~ hadn't been **4** ~~had bought~~ bought; ~~always wanted~~ had always wanted **5** ~~she just finished~~ she had just finished **6** ~~I have been cleaning~~ I had been cleaning

Speaking | Part 3

In Speaking Part 3, candidates have to first discuss various options as solutions to a problem or as opportunities to do something, and second, to decide which option(s) to choose. This part tests students' ability to interact over several minutes in discussion, their ability to exchange ideas and opinions, agree and disagree, suggest, negotiate, etc.

Students need to listen carefully to each other and react to the other student's ideas, as well as come up with their own.

They should aim to have a balanced discussion rather than trying to speak more than their partner.

1 ***As a warmer*** With books closed, elicit what reasons there are for organising school trips. (Possible answers: To give students wider experiences, to learn a language or learn about a culture, to form stronger relationships with their fellow students, to have some adventure, to have a break from school, to teach things in a practical setting, etc.)

Put students in small groups. Ask them to say what school trips they have been on, which ones they enjoyed most, and which ones they did not enjoy so much.

With books open, go through the Exam information box before moving to the task and eliciting what each type of trip involves, e.g. seeing the important monuments, taking exercise and living outdoors, etc.

2 Before they listen, ask students to predict what benefits the two students will mention about the first three options. They can then listen to check if they were correct and take notes.

Answers
A city sightseeing tour: you learn about architecture and history, other cultures and visit somewhere different.
A weekend camping trip in the mountains: you have exciting experiences and adventures, and learn to be independent, learn to work together to solve problems, learn teamwork, educational.
A beach activity day: you learn something from doing different sports and activities.

CD 1 Track 10

Miguel: Shall we start with this one?

Antonia: OK.

Miguel: How do you think doing a sightseeing tour of a city might be good for students?

Antonia: I think you can learn a lot about architecture and history and things like that.

Miguel: Yes, and also you can visit somewhere very different and learn about other cultures.

Antonia: Right. What about this sort of activity holiday in the mountains? I think it can give young people exciting experiences and adventures, things they don't get in their everyday lives.

Miguel: Yes, and they learn to be more independent because they're away from home and their families, don't you think?

Antonia: I think that's right. Also, they learn to work together to solve problems, so it's good for learning teamwork.

Miguel: That's an important point, because if the school's organising the trip, it should be educational, shouldn't it? I mean, students have got to be learning something. And the beach activity day: what about that?

Antonia: It sounds great, doesn't it? And I think just by doing sports and activities they don't normally do at school, students learn something.

Miguel: I agree.

3 Point out that it is important to have a natural conversation and to encourage partners to share ideas with simple questions like these.

Answers
1 Shall; this one **2** think **3** What about
4 don't you **5** about that

4 Pronunciation: intonation

1 You can point out that intonation may indicate many other things, such as how interested the speaker is, surprise, certainty or uncertainty, and that it forms an integral part of the speaker's message.

CD 1 Track 11

1 How do you think a sightseeing tour might be good ↘for students?
2 I think you can learn a lot about archi↗tecture and ↗history and things ↘like that.
3 Yes, and also you can visit somewhere very dif↘ferent and learn about other cul↘tures.
4 What about this sort of ac↗tivity holiday in the moun↘tains?
5 I think it can give young people exciting ex↗periences and ad↗ventures, things they don't get in their everyday ↘lives.

Answers
See Track 11.

2 ***Alternative treatment*** If you wish, play the sentences again and ask students to repeat either in chorus or individually.

You can also ask them just to repeat the underlined words.

3 ***Alternative treatment*** When students are ready to speak, tell them they should listen carefully to their partners. If their intonation does not fall, it indicates that they have not finished speaking, so they should wait till they have finished.

5 Ask students to change partners for this exercise so that they have a chance to talk to someone who may have different ideas.

6 Tell students that thinking about what strategies will produce the best results in this part will help them to have a useful, constructive discussion and help them to achieve a higher score in the exam.

Suggested answers
1 N – There is not time – you need to reach a decision in one minute.
2 Y – It gets the discussion started and your partner involved.
3 N – It prevents further discussion.
4 Y – This is a possible way of creating more discussion.
5 Y – It creates further discussion.
6 N – You only have a minute and you will get higher marks if you can have a natural conversation.

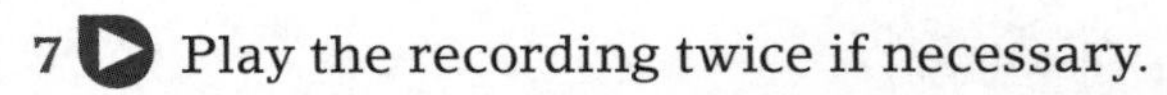
7 Play the recording twice if necessary.

Answers
Miguel does 2; Antonia does 4; Irene and Nikolai both do 5.

CD 1 Track 12

Miguel and Antonia

Miguel: Well, Antonia, in my opinion, the best choice for the trip is the camping and walking activity in the mountains, because it will be an adventure for everyone, and if it goes well, everyone will enjoy it. What do you think?

Antonia: Hmm, I think your suggestion would be fine if the weather is good, but no one will enjoy it if it rains all the time, and it's a lot of responsibility for the teachers who are supervising the trip. I think the beach-activities trip is a better option because at least the kids will be staying in a hostel if the weather turns bad.

Irene and Nikolai

Irene: OK, I think we should choose the theme park because all teenagers enjoy the thrill of a theme park, and it gives everyone plenty to talk about and discuss before and after they go.

Nikolai: Yes, I think you're right, but I think we should also consider the visit to the museum because that might be more popular with the teachers, and we have to take their preferences into consideration as well.

Irene: Hmm, you might be right, but I think we should put the students' tastes first because it is their trip.

Nikolai: Maybe, but they can go to a theme park in their own time.

Irene: Yes, of course they can, but sometimes it's important to do these activities as a school group.

Extension idea Ask: *Which strategy do you think worked best in this task? Why?*

8 **Answers**
1 a **2** a **3** b **4** e **5** e **6** d **7** c

Extension idea Print out and photocopy the script from the Teacher's Resources CD-ROM. Ask students to find the phrases in the script and listen to the speakers again.

They should then take turns to read the sentences containing the phrases aloud, concentrating on stress and intonation.

9 Although they only have a minute for this in the exam, allow students a little longer on this occasion, so they can practise the strategies they chose.

Round up with the whole class by asking what strategies they used, which options they decided on, and why.

Extension idea: Ask students to change partners and do the task again.

When they have finished, ask them if they decided on a different option the second time and if so, why.

Writing | Part 2 A report

1 ***As a warmer*** With books closed, tell students in small groups to discuss:

- *Why do schools organise excursions for their students?*
- *What do you like and dislike about school excursions?*

With books open, ask: *Have you ever had to write a report in your own language about a school excursion?*

Tell students it is important to underline key ideas in the question first to make sure they answer the question completely.

Suggested underlining
one-day excursion, local place of interest, what you did, why, the day, a success

2 Ask students to make some notes while, or after, they discuss.

3 Tell students that they will score marks for using a range of tenses and other grammar appropriately in their writing.

Answers
1 took **2** went **3** was **4** had been **5** rode
6 were **7** took **8** had operated **9** was **10** were
11 enjoyed **12** learned **13** had **14** found

Extension idea Ask students: *Would you enjoy an excursion like this one? Why? / Why not?*

4 Tell students that:

- reports should have a clear structure and format
- they should use a range of appropriate grammar
- they should answer all parts of the task.

Answers
1 Yes – *Excursion to London*
2 Three – Each has a heading: *Purpose of trip, What we did, Comments*
3 Three – a break from normal lessons, to see the London Eye and do a tour of the Globe Theatre
4 The activities were interesting, different, everyone enjoyed something, plenty of opportunities to practise English – motivating.

5 ***Extension idea*** When students have finished, ask them to change partners and compare their plans and ideas with another student. If you wish, round up afterwards with the whole class.

6 Tell students that this task should take them about 40 minutes. If you wish, this can be done for homework.

Tell them that when they write, they should follow their plan carefully: good planning is key to successful writing.

For more on writing reports, refer students to page 191 (Writing reference – Reports).

Sample answer
See the model in Exercise 3 in the Student's Book.

Food, glorious food

Unit objectives

- **Reading and Use of English Part 6:** identifying paragraph topics; using cohesive devices and referencing to help fill the gaps
- **Reading and Use of English Part 1:** introduction to task type; differentiating between words with similar meanings
- **Writing Part 2:** structuring and writing a review; deciding on content; using adjectives to comment
- **Listening Part 4:** introduction to task type; identifying and underlining key ideas in questions
- **Speaking Part 4:** introduction to task type; expressing opinions and supporting them with examples and reasons; balancing opinions
- **Pronunciation:** grouping words and pausing (1)
- **Vocabulary:** confusion between *food, dish* and *meal*; adjective collocations with *food, dish* and *meal*; adjectives to describe restaurants and food
- **Grammar:** *so* and *such*; *too* and *enough*

Starting off

1 ***As a warmer*** With books closed, ask students in small groups: *Can you think of five ways the food we eat will change in the future?*

Give students three or four minutes to discuss the question, then round up with the whole class and discuss.

With books open, say: *Look at the photos. Do you eat any of these things already? Did you mention any of these things in your discussion?*

Answers
1 e **2** b **3** d **4** c **5** a

2 **Answers**
1 Photo 5 **2** Photo 1 **3** Photo 2 **4** Photo 3 **5** Photo 4

3 ***Alternative treatment 1*** Ask students to work alone and decide how they feel about the questions. They then walk round the class asking other students their opinions and trying to find which student in the class agrees most exactly with them.

Alternative treatment 2 You can treat this as a class discussion.

Extension idea Write these questions on the board and ask the class to discuss them (this will lead into Reading and Use of English Part 6 which follows):

- *Why is it important to eat good-quality food?*
- *How important is it to know about what we eat?*
- *What ways are there of getting information about the food we eat?*

Reading and Use of English | Part 6

As a warmer Tell students they are going to read an article about food in a school in the United States. Ask:

- *What do you think students in the United States typically eat?*
- *From watching films and TV, how are American eating habits different from eating habits in this country / your own country?*

1 **Note:** School meals vary round the USA. Many students complain about their quality and go out to fast-food restaurants; most US schools have vending machines selling snacks and soft drinks; there is a lot of public discussion about the quality of school food and obesity amongst young people; in some poor districts, school breakfasts are also provided.

Suggested answers
Benefits: learning to do these things, learning about nutrition, becoming independent, health benefits

2 Remind students that this task requires them to understand the structure of the text. Making a note of the topic of each paragraph helps them to do this. Give students six minutes to do this exercise. They can then work in pairs and compare their notes.

Suggested answers
Para. 2: the campaign and the reasons for it
Para. 3: the food and where it comes from
Para. 4: classroom activities in the garden
Para. 5: classroom activities in the kitchen
Para. 6: Teo's opinion
Para. 7: the general aim of the garden

3 Elicit why the words and phrases highlighted as examples in Sentence A refer to other parts of the text:

- *How does 'this garden' refer to other parts of the text?* (Answer: It's a garden which has been previously mentioned.)
- *According to your notes, which paragraphs talk about the garden?*
- *What does 'the answer' refer to?* (Answer: A question asked previously)
- *Which paragraph asks and answers questions?*

Suggested underlining
C One lesson **D** The problem, these projects
E These two projects **F** We, in this small space
G Lessons like this one

Extension idea After you have rounded up with the whole class which words/phrases should be highlighted, ask them to work in pairs and, without reading the text, say what each highlighted word/phrase may refer to.

4 When students have finished, tell them to read the whole text again quickly to check their answers. Give them three minutes for this.

They then compare their answers with a partner.

Answers
1 G **2** E **3** F **4** B **5** C **6** A

5 Encourage students to support their answers with examples from their own experience.

Vocabulary

food, dish and meal

1 ***As a warmer*** To highlight the difference, write *lunch, eggs* and *mushroom omelette* on the board and ask students which is food, which a dish and which a meal.

Answers
1 food; meals **2** food; dishes **3** meal

2 If these are mistakes your students make, you could suggest that they keep a section of their notebooks to write down their typical vocabulary mistakes (many frequent mistakes by candidates are dealt with throughout this course). They can then refer to them and revise the differences and corrections easily before the exam.

Answers
2 ~~meals~~ dishes **3** ~~food~~ dish **4** ~~meal~~ food
5 ~~meals~~ food **6** ~~food~~ dish **7** ~~dishes~~ meals

3 EP Students can check words and phrases from this exercise using the word list from the Teacher's Resources CD-ROM.

Answers
1 food **2** food **3** meal; dish **4** meal

4 EP

Answers
2 food shortages **3** heavy/filling meal **4** food source **5** convenience food **6** balanced meals
7 food supply **8** organic food

Extension idea Ask students to discuss these questions in small groups:

- *Do/Did you eat at school or college? If so, what is/was the food like?*
- *What is your favourite meal of the day?*
- *Which is your favourite dish? Who prepares it for you?*

5 Remind students that this is similar to Speaking Part 3. Ask them to look back at the Speaking section on page 37 in Unit 3 to remind themselves of how to do this type of task.

If you wish to replicate exam conditions, give them two minutes to do the first part and one minute to do the second part.

Extension idea When they have finished, ask students to change partners and summarise what they decided.

Grammar

so and such

1 After students have done this exercise, go through the notes in the Language reference section on page 175 (*so* and *such*) with them.

Answers
1 such a; So **2** such a; so **3** such

2

Answers
1 such **2** so **3** such a **4** so **5** so **6** such a

Extension idea When they have finished, ask students to write four sentences of their own using *so, such* and *such a(n)*.

3 Remind students that it is important to be able to find and correct their own mistakes.

Answers
1 ~~such~~ so **2** ~~a so much~~ such **3** correct **4** ~~so~~ such
5 ~~so~~ such a **6** ~~such~~ so **7** correct **8** ~~so~~ such

4 Remind students they may have to make changes to vocabulary as well as grammar when doing this task.

Answers
1 never eaten such a good **2** so quickly that we **3** answered the question so well/excellently **4** with so little food **5** had so much fun at **6** make so much noise

Listening | Part 4

As a warmer With books closed, ask students:

- *Where are the best places in this town / your town for people your age to meet after school or in your free time?*
- *What sort of things do people do there?*

1 When students have done the exercise in the book, round up answers with the whole class.

2 Listening Part 4 primarily tests students' ability to understand speakers' attitudes and opinions. Students need to hear the whole of an exchange before choosing an answer, which may be expressed as a main idea, or as gist, or as a specific detail. Each question is usually marked by a question from the interviewer so that students know which question they should be focusing on at any one time.

Before students read the questions, go through the Exam information box with them. Point out that in the exam, they will have one minute to read the questions.

To help focus their listening, they should underline key ideas in the questions but not in the options A–C. (If they underline words in the options, they will be trying to focus on too much information and may get confused. Also they will be focusing on wrong answers which may not be mentioned at all in the recording.)

Give them a minute to do this.

Suggested underlining
1 started, because **2** most important, chose the site **3** décor **4** How, behave with, customers **5** purpose, back room **6** food, should be **7** What, parents like

3 ▶ Before they listen, tell students that in this part, they should also listen carefully to the interviewer's questions, as these will usually indicate which question is going to be answered next.

After playing the recording twice, give students some time to check their answers and then compare them in pairs.

Answers
1 B **2** C **3** C **4** A **5** B **6** B **7** A

CD 1 Track 13

Interviewer: Hi! Today I'm talking to Cherry Smith, owner of Cherry's Café, a well-known spot for youngsters in our town. Cherry – can you tell us a little bit about your café and why you started it?

Cherry: Sure. I was working in one of the local supermarkets – it was always my ambition from when I was quite little to be working with people, and [1]I noticed that there were lots of secondary-school kids coming in to buy snacks and soft drinks and things and just hanging around and I thought, 'Poor things, they've got too much free time and they're not eating well enough and [1]they need somewhere they can hang out.' So I came up with this idea of a café where kids could just spend their free time and [1]I could make a living out of it as well.

Interviewer: Great! So did you choose this site for your café because it's between the two local schools?

Cherry: Well, that was one consideration, but I thought [2]it was essential to have a place which was just that bit bigger than the other cafés in the area and I found this place with an extra room at the back where customers can go and not be seen from the street by passers-by and you know everyone from the two schools does go past.

Interviewer: And, Cherry, did you need to put much thought into the interior decoration?

Cherry: Yeah, lots. [3]I was really wanting a place where kids can come at lunchtime or after school and feel comfortable, so comfy chairs, warm colours, things that make them feel at home. Nothing fragile because we don't want to be replacing furniture every five minutes. I get them to help out a bit too, so, you know, they help wipe tables and sweep up from time to time, otherwise we wouldn't manage.

Interviewer: So, your customers are mainly young people from the local schools. Do they give you any problems?

Cherry: They're almost all from the local schools and not really. They behave quite well really, and I say 'quite' because they are young, so they're going to be noisy and want to play around a bit, but they're never rude to me or rough. I just like people and young people especially. [4]I think everyone's interesting so I try to find out things about them and I pull their legs sometimes – we have a good laugh – like they're friends. And they react to that. I don't impose discipline or anything, 'cos it's not like lessons. And that doesn't mean I'm always going to look happy – I have my 'off' days, just like anyone else.

Interviewer: You mentioned a room at the back as being important. Why's that?

Cherry: Well, I want kids to come here and feel that it's like another home. Somewhere they can just be themselves, so [5]the back room is the sort of quiet room where they can just sit down and read, or do their internet stuff, or finish their homework, or have a quiet chat. You know, young people need these sorts of places where they can be quiet if they want to be, but have company if they want it too.

Interviewer: Fantastic. How about food? Do you just give your customers whatever they want?

Cherry: Well, [6]I think it's important to offer young people food they can afford. I mean, I don't worry about if it's good for them or not. We do serve things like hamburgers and chips, but we also offer salads and fresh vegetables. You'd be surprised how popular they are. I don't do the cooking – Mikey does that 'cos I don't have enough time. They're all simple dishes but they can be quite filling.

Interviewer: Great! And finally, Cherry, what do parents think of your café? Do you get any comments?

Cherry: Actually, I don't see too many parents, but the odd comment comes back. I think [7]what they really appreciate is that you know, their kids are in a friendly place where they feel happy. Parents sometimes sort of jokingly complain when their kids tell them they don't cook as well as Mikey. And you know, in the end, this café is a cost for the parents, but I think they think it's worth it.

Interviewer: Cherry, thanks.

Cherry: Thank you.

Extension idea Print out and photocopy the recording script from the Teacher's Resources CD-ROM.

Play the recording again and ask students to check their answers as they follow the script.

Write these phrasal verbs and expressions on the board and ask students to find them in the script:

hanging around *hang out* *make a living*
put thought into *help out* *play around* *pull their legs*

Ask students in pairs to look at the context and decide (approximately) what each phrase means.

Ask students to work alone and write three or four sentences using some of the phrases from the list. They can then compare these with a partner or read them out to the whole class.

4 ***Extension idea*** While students are discussing, ask them to make a few notes.

When they have finished, ask them to form small groups with other partners and to take turns to present the ideas and opinions they have just discussed.

Grammar

too and enough

1

Answers
1 too much; enough **2** too **3** enough **4** enough **5** too many

Extension idea Ask students in pairs or small groups to work out the rules for when to use *too* and *enough*. When they have finished, ask them to check their ideas by looking at the Language reference section on page 176.

2

Answers
1 too many; enough **2** enough **3** too **4** too **5** enough

3 Remind students to look out for and correct these mistakes when they are speaking and writing.

Answers
1 ~~the food wasn't enough~~ there wasn't enough food **2** ~~not too much good~~ not very good **3** ~~money enough~~ enough money **4** ~~enough comfortable~~ comfortable enough **5** ~~too much long~~ (much) too long **6** ~~doing too hard work~~ working too hard / doing too much hard work **7** ~~too much tasty~~ very tasty **8** ~~too much expensive~~ (much) too expensive

4

Answers
1 is too expensive for **2** enough petrol to get **3** was too astonished by **4** was not / wasn't warm enough for

5 To make this exercise more enjoyable, encourage students to exaggerate their complaints and to give details.

Extension idea Ask students to change pairs and give an account of the birthday party and why it was such a disaster.

This may be a suitable moment to do the photocopiable activity on the Teacher's Resources CD-ROM.

Speaking | Part 4

Speaking Part 4 tests students' ability to express opinions and to justify them by supporting them with reasons, explanations and examples.

As a warmer With books closed, ask students in pairs to answer this question: *Do you think fast food is bad for you?*

Round up ideas with the whole class.

1 With books open, go through the Exam information box.

Ask students to quickly look at Martyna's and Miguel's answers and say which ideas they expressed and which they agree with.

When students look at the words/phrases in bold in Martyna's and Miguel's answers, point out that the words/phrases are examples of appropriate topic vocabulary, including phrasal verbs.

Answers
b balanced diet **c** cut down **d** junk food
e dairy products **f** live on **g** lifestyle

2 Point out to students that the words and phrases they need to fill the gaps help to make fairly long, complex sentences and that they will also score higher marks for using more complex grammatical structures appropriately in the exam.

Answers
1 in other words **2** because **3** On the other hand
4 then **5** but **6** which **7** what

CD 1 Track 14

Examiner: Do you think fast food is bad for you?

Martyna: I think it depends. I think the most important thing / is to have a balanced diet, / in other words, you eat a variety of / vegetables, / meat, / cereals and so on. I'm not sure it matters so much / how long it takes to prepare, / because I think fast food is / just / food which is prepared quickly. On the other hand, / if you just live on / what's it called / junk food, / for instance hamburgers and pizzas and things like that, / then you probably need to cut down / and have a more balanced diet.

Examiner: And Miguel, what do you think?

Miguel: I agree with Martyna. / I think it's fine to eat fast food occasionally, / but you have to balance it with other things like / fresh fruit and / vegetables which are in season and / cut down on dairy products and fat. / Also I think that what you eat is only one part of a / healthy lifestyle.

Martyna: I agree.

3 Tell students that in this part of the exam, it is important that they justify the opinions which they express, and this can be done by giving reasons and examples. It is not necessary in the exam to give a balanced answer, but students who can do this will further impress the examiner.

Answers
1 in other words **2** because **3** for instance, like
4 but, on the other hand

Extension idea Ask students to think of other words/phrases they can use to introduce reasons and examples. You can write what they suggest on the board.

(Suggested answers: reasons: *for that reason, because of (that), that's why*; examples: *such as, for example*)

4 Pronunciation: grouping words and pausing (1)

1 Tell students that grouping words together in chunks and pausing naturally between the chunks is an essential part of fluency and natural speech rhythms. Pausing in places where it is natural to pause helps the listener to understand. While there are no rules, it is natural to pause between groups of words which form a 'chunk' of meaning. As students grow more fluent, the chunks may become longer, depending on the complexity of what they are talking about and how much they have to think and choose their words.

Answers
See recording script for Track 15.

CD 1 Track 15

Examiner: How can families benefit from eating together?

Miguel: Well, / the important thing is not eating, / it's spending time together / so that they can talk about / what they have been doing during the day. / They get the chance to / exchange opinions / and make plans as well, / because everyone can contribute and / that's what makes a / rich, / meaningful family life. / Children learn ideas and attitudes from their parents, / while parents keep up to date with their children / and what they are thinking and doing.

Examiner: And Martyna, do you agree?

Martyna: Yes, I do. / And also I think people cook better / when they are cooking for several people / than when they are just cooking for themselves, / so that as a result, / people who eat together / eat more healthily.

Extension idea Ask students in pairs to take turns to answer this question: *Do you agree with Miguel's and Martyna's answers to the question 'How can families benefit from eating together?'*?

2 Tell the student who is listening to count how many times their partner pauses. When they finish, they can also give feedback about whether they think their partner pauses too often, or not often enough.

They should then change roles and read the dialogue again.

3 If necessary, play the recording twice.

Answers
See recording script for Track 15.

4 Students who are listening should again check where their partner pauses and how natural it sounds.

5 and 6 When students have finished, round up ideas from the whole class.

7 ***Alternative treatment*** As a whole-class activity, ask one of the questions to one student, e.g. *Maria, do you think that fast food is bad for you?*

Maria answers and then asks someone else in the class: *Do you agree with me?*

The next student answers and then asks someone in the class: *Do you agree with me?* until the subject is exhausted. Then another question is chosen.

This way, students have to listen carefully to the opinions expressed as well as offer their own.

Reading and Use of English | Part 1

Reading and Use of English Part 1 tests students' knowledge of lexis, particularly choosing the correct option for a context from a group of words with similar meanings. Students choose on the basis of a dependent preposition, gerund, infinitive or other grammatical feature, knowledge of collocations and set phrases or expressions. Undoubtedly the best preparation for this task is extended experience of the language, especially extended reading and listening, which builds up students' internalised language knowledge.

1 ***As a warmer*** Ask students:

- *Do you like food from other countries? Which countries? Why?*
- *What things are important when choosing somewhere to eat out when you're celebrating something important?*

Give students one minute to skim the text.

Answers
The surroundings, the service, the food, the price

2 Elicit why B is the correct answer in the example, i.e. *checked, tested* and *proved* have wrong meanings. Elicit answers for questions 1–3 with the whole class.

Answers
1 C **2** B **3** C **4** B **5** A **6** D **7** C **8** A

3 ***Extension idea*** When students have finished discussing, ask them to change groups and present their ideas to their new group. Each student should speak for about a minute.

Writing | Part 2 A review

1 ***As a warmer*** Ask students:

- *How do you find out if a book is worth reading, a video game worth buying, a film worth seeing or a restaurant worth visiting?*
- *Do you ever read reviews and, if so, where do you read them?*
- *Do you ever read reviews before you buy things online?*
- *Has anyone here ever written a review for an online shopping site, e.g. Amazon?*
- *How useful would the review in Reading and Use of English Part 1 be if you were looking for a restaurant?*

Ask them to recommend publications or websites for reading reviews.

Suggested underlining
local English-language newspaper, recommend, local restaurant, café or snack bar, review, what, place, food, like, why, family, enjoy eating there

2 ***Alternative treatment*** Ask students to decide which of the elements is essential, which optional.

Answers
2 a, b, c, d, f, h, i

Extension idea Ask students to look back to the review in Reading and Use of English Part 1 and write a paragraph plan for it. (Suggested answer: Paragraph 1: when visited, type of restaurant, general comment; Paragraph 2: interior and waiters – comparison with other restaurants; Paragraph 3: the food and the price; Paragraph 4: a general recommendation)

3 **Suggested answers**
the waiters / the service: rushed, welcoming, informative, cheerful, exceptional, satisfactory, superb
the interior: airy, cosy, modern, attractive, cheerful, colourful, elegant, exclusive, original, welcoming
the food and menu: delicious, fresh, satisfying, tasty, wonderful, attractive, colourful, delightful, elegant, exceptional, original, raw, satisfactory, superb, well-balanced
the price: reasonable, competitive
the restaurant in general: modern, attractive, colourful, delightful, exceptional, elegant, exclusive, original, superb, welcoming

4 EP If you have printed out and photocopied the word list from the Teacher's Resources CD-ROM for this unit, students can use it to help them complete the table.

Extension idea Ask students to add two adjectives of their own to each column. You can then round these up with the whole class.

5 **Suggested underlining**
college magazine, favourite restaurant, café or snack bar, review, 'Free Time' section, what, place, like, why, recommend it

6 Ask students to work alone to write their plans and note down their ideas.

7 When they have finished discussing, ask them to look back through the unit and the word list (if they have it) and note down any vocabulary they would like to use.

8 Tell students that this task should take them about 40 minutes. If you wish, this can be done for homework.

→ For more on writing reviews, you can refer students to page 192 (Writing reference – Reviews).

Vocabulary and grammar review Unit 3

1 **1** journey **2** trip **3** travel **4** way **5** journey **6** way **7** trip **8** journey

2 **1** while I was visiting **2** I had lost **3** used to go to school **4** she was still going to **5** had never met **6** used to be more

3 **1** considerable **2** exclusive **3** dramatic **4** unacceptable **5** disorganised **6** unhelpful **7** remaining **8** preferable

Vocabulary and grammar review Unit 4

1 **1** meal **2** food **3** dish **4** food **5** dish **6** food/meal **7** meal **8** food

2 **1** too hot (for us) to **2** slowly enough (for us) to **3** was so full (that) **4** such delicious food that **5** cook well enough **6** such a long time / so much time

3 **1** filling **2** convenience **3** increasingly **4** organisations **5** discourage **6** balanced **7** disappearance **8** choice

5 Study time

Unit objectives

- **Reading and Use of English Part 7:** identifying main ideas in questions; underlining evidence in the text
- **Reading and Use of English Part 3:** forming nouns from verbs; deciding what type of word is required
- **Writing Part 1:** writing an essay; writing opening paragraphs; using linking words and phrases
- **Listening Part 1:** listening for gist and specific information
- **Speaking Part 1:** talking about studying and educational experiences; giving reasons in answers; volunteering information; showing an interested attitude
- **Pronunciation:** word stress (2)
- **Vocabulary:** words connected with education: *tutor, research,* etc.; phrasal verbs, e.g. *get away with, get over, live up to,* etc.; confusion between *find out, get to know, know, learn, teach* and *study*; *attend, join, take part* and *assist*; collocations to give reasons for studying abroad; forming nouns from verbs
- **Grammar:** zero, first and second conditionals; forming indirect questions

Starting off

As a warmer With books closed, ask students, working alone, to complete this sentence with three things which are true for them:

I'm studying in order to …

They then work in small groups and compare their aims and give reasons for them.

Alternative treatment Before students answer the questions in the book, write these phrases on the board:

playing an instrument   revision   field trip
sports team   cultural trip

Ask students to match the phrases with the photos. ((top left) revision; (top middle) field trip; (top right) team sports; (middle) cultural trip; (bottom) playing an instrument)

Listening | Part 1

1 

Answers
1 h **2** d **3** b **4** a **5** i **6** e **7** f **8** c **9** g

Extension idea To activate the vocabulary, write the following prompts on the board:

- *tutor / help?*
- *ever done research?*
- *good learner?*
- *mark your homework?*
- *exam / like / pass?*
- *plan / sit / exam?*
- *course requirements / for this subject?*
- *job prospects / in future?*

Ask students to work in pairs and use three of the prompts to write questions which they will then ask others in the class. (Possible questions: *How can a tutor help you to study? Have you ever done any research? What makes a good language learner? How often do teachers mark your homework? What exam would you like to pass? Are you planning to sit any exams? What are the course requirements for this subject? What do you think your job prospects are for the future?*)

Students then walk round the class asking and answering questions.

2 Tell students that even when they underline most of the words in a question, this is useful as it:

- makes them think about what each question is asking
- serves as a reminder when they look at the question again.

Suggested underlining
1 How does he feel, now **2** What, problem **3** What, like most **4** What, main benefit **5** Why, talking **6** What surprised her, school **7** think about, lesson **8** What, advice about

3 After listening, give students time to check their answers and then to compare them with a partner's.

Answers
1 C **2** B **3** B **4** A **5** A **6** C **7** C **8** B

Extension idea 1 Print out and photocopy the recording script from the Teacher's Resources CD-ROM. Ask students to check their answers and underline the words which gave them the answers. If you wish, you can play the recording again while they check.

Extension idea 2 After doing the listening exercise and the vocabulary exercise which follows, ask students to work in pairs and:

- write one multiple-choice question like those in the exercise, and one short monologue or dialogue to go with it. They first read their question and then their monologue/dialogue to the class, who should choose the answer
- ask students to include one or two of the phrases from the vocabulary exercise in their script.

CD 1 Track 16

Presenter: One. You overhear a student talking about a course he has been doing.

Will: Actually, at the beginning of term, I was a bit lost. You know, my family has only just moved to this country, so I was new in this school, and I felt that everyone else knew more about the subject than I did. Listening to them, I got the impression that some of them felt this particular course was a bit of a waste of time. In my case, I was having problems not just with the language but also with the ideas. But I managed to get over all that and, in fact, [1]the course has lived up to my original expectations, so I feel all the hard work's been worth it. I mean, we've got an exam next week, which I expected to feel a bit anxious about, but in fact I'm feeling fine about it.

Presenter: Two. You hear a student complaining about a problem she has had.

Mike: Oh, Helena! What's up?

Helena: Do you know what just happened? I was given an essay to write at the beginning of the month and I spent lots of time researching it. Anyway, Valerie – you know her – she came round to my place and while she was there she must have copied all my notes! All my research! I only found out in my tutorial just now when the tutor handed my essay back to me. [2]He said he couldn't mark it because my essay repeated all the same key points that Valerie had made in hers. I'm absolutely furious, and she's going to get away with it, too!

Presenter: Three. You hear a student at a language school in Japan.

Boy: So, what are you doing here in Japan?

Girl: I'm learning Japanese at a language school. I go to classes for just two hours a day, which is good because I learn Japanese from Japanese teachers, and then I'm free to practise it during the rest of the day.

Boy: That sounds a good idea.

Girl: It is. You see, it's not all academic work. They also organise lots of other things for us learners to take part in after school. [3]There are clubs we can join if we're interested, and they really are the best part. For example, I'm also doing a karate course taught in Japanese, which is great fun. I'm learning something completely different in the language I'm studying and I'm getting to know lots of local people.

Boy: Fantastic!

Girl: Yes, if you speak a bit of the language, it's much easier to make friends.

Presenter: Four. You hear an interview with a student who is thinking of studying abroad.

Sandra: I'm not sure whether I'll study abroad. I've been thinking of going to an Italian university and studying international business for a year – that's if I get through the admission process. The trouble is partly that if I went, it might make it more difficult for me to get a good pass in my exams back home. On the other hand, [4]I think the opportunity to live abroad for a year would be extremely educational, because I'd learn about the Italian way of life and way of thinking. Trouble is, I'd have to leave all my friends and probably live on my own, and I'm not sure if I'm ready for that.

Presenter: Five. You overhear the director of a school talking to students.

Peter: Now, [5]just a few things I need to point out to new students. First, you're expected to attend all your lessons and do the work your teachers give you. If for any reason you can't make it to a lesson, remember to let your teacher know. If your teacher has to cancel a lesson or put it off, he or she'll try to tell you in advance. Also, please remember that most of what you study here is very practical, and you have to do one big piece of project work during the year. You're allowed to do it in groups, and if you work with other students, you'll probably find it easier. Apart from that, you'll also have to sit an end-of-year exam, so it's important to study hard throughout the year.

Presenter: Six. You hear a girl leaving a message about her first day at a new school.

Carrie: Hi, Mum! I'm just calling to say I'm back and I'm still alive! You know how worried I was because I wouldn't know anyone, and you said there'd be lots of other kids in the same situation – and you were right, so we all sort of mixed in. Classes were fine – you know, the usual sort of stuff you do on the first day like course requirements and so on. One or two of the teachers might turn out to be monsters, but most seem fine. Oh, and [6]the classrooms are nice, very bright and lots of technology like electronic screens and we're all connected up with wifi and stuff, [7]so a lot better than I expected.

Presenter: Seven. You hear two students, a boy and a girl, talking about a lesson.

Jan: Hi, Max. So you got into trouble in maths again for staring out of the window!

Max: Yeah! I reckon Mr Drew's got it in for me! I mean, you don't have to look at the teacher to be listening to him.

Jan: So, unlike most of us, you were actually finding the lesson useful, you mean?

Max: Sure. Mr Drew knows what he's talking about, and there are some interesting concepts, but unfortunately [7]it's all rather chaotic, and it takes him such a long time to get to the stuff we really need. [7]His classes could do with a bit more planning, in my opinion.

Jan: Hmm, perhaps that's why the rest of us all get lost, while you're staring at the kids outside – and taking it all in!

Presenter: Eight. You hear a teacher talking to a student.

Teacher: Well, [8]it's fine to study history or archaeology if that's the area you're planning to work in when you finish, but you must remember, you'll only find the sort of job you want in research if you get a really good degree – and the job itself won't be very well paid either.

Girl: I know.

Teacher: I mean, you've got a good brain and [8]if you applied yourself, you could study anything. I'd hate to think of you looking back in 20 years' time and thinking, I wish I'd studied IT or accountancy or something with better job prospects.

Vocabulary

Phrasal verbs

1 EP ***Alternative treatment*** Ask students in pairs or small groups to try to remember the context for each verb.

Print out and photocopy the recording script for Track 16 from the Teacher's Resources CD-ROM for students to check the context and the meanings.

> **Answers**
> **1** c **2** a **3** e **4** g **5** h **6** b **7** d **8** f

2

> **Answers**
> **1** put off **2** gets away with **3** handed; back; gets over **4** live up to; looks back **5** turned out; point / pointed / have pointed out

Extension idea Ask students in pairs to choose three phrasal verbs from Exercise 1 and write three sentences with a gap where each phrasal verb should be (like the ones in this exercise).

They then exchange sentences with another pair and write the correct phrasal verbs in the gaps.

find out, get to know, know, learn, teach and *study; attend, join, take part* and *assist*

3 Tell students to copy the words into their notebooks and to take care to use them correctly when speaking or writing.

> **Answers**
> **1** studying **2** found out **3** learn **4** learn **5** taught **6** getting to know **7** take part **8** join **9** attend

4

> **Answers**
> **1** studying **2** got to know **3** study **4** learned **5** find out **6** know **7** taught **8** assist **9** joined **10** taken part

Grammar

Zero, first and second conditionals

1 After students have done the exercise, ask them to check their answers in the Language reference section on page 164 (Conditionals).

Answers
a 3, 5, 6 **b** 2, 4 **c** 1

2 ***Alternative treatment*** Ask students to work in pairs, cover the endings (a–j) and complete each sentence in any way they like. When they have finished, they compare their ideas with the endings in the Student's Book.

Answers
1 h **2** f **3** j **4** g **5** a **6** e **7** c **8** d **9** i (or f) **10** b

Extension idea To fix the relationship between tenses in each type of conditional, ask students to say which type of conditional each sentence is. (**1** 1st **2** 2nd **3** zero **4** 1st **5** 1st **6** 1st **7** 2nd **8** 2nd **9** 2nd **10** zero)

3 Tell students it is important to remember which tense comes in each part of each conditional.

Tell them they should not avoid using conditionals, but practise using them and refer to the Language reference section when necessary to check they are using them correctly. Examiners will recognise and give credit for attempts to use more complex language appropriately; candidates are not penalised for mistakes due to 'ambition'.

Answers
1 ~~say~~ said **2** ~~live~~ lived **3** ~~study~~ studied OR ~~would~~ will **4** ~~we'll have~~ we have **5** ~~you'll have~~ you have **6** ~~will be~~ is **7** ~~buy~~ bought OR ~~would~~ will **8** ~~take~~ took OR ~~would~~ will; ~~could~~ can **9** ~~you'll decide~~ you decide **10** ~~travelled~~ travel OR ~~will~~ would

4

Answers
1 you assist (us) with the **2** if you join **3** would take part in **4** will have to put off **5** better unless your teacher pointed **6** I get over my cold

5 Encourage students to give reasons for their answers and to discuss them.

Extension idea Ask students to add two or three more questions of their own to the list and ask these as well.

This would be a suitable moment to do the photocopiable activity on the Teacher's Resources CD-ROM.

Reading and Use of English | Part 7

As a warmer With books closed, ask students in small groups:

- *What problems can students have when going to school in another country?*
- *Which are serious problems and which are not so serious?*

Find out if any students in the class have done an educational exchange, or know someone who has. Ask them to talk a little about the experience.

1 When students open their books, the third question gives students an opportunity to practise second conditionals.

2 Suggested answers
1 unfamiliar food and a difficult/strange host family; food the student doesn't like **2** not having friends; feeling lonely **3** not knowing their way around; feeling lost **4** difficulty understanding people / the teacher / the lessons

2 Tell students that in some questions, they may have to underline most of the words. Remind them that they should spend time studying and understanding the questions before reading the texts. This will avoid constantly going back and forth between the texts and the questions.

Suggested underlining
1 surprised, different approach to education **2** cooperating, host family **3** more adult as a result **4** equip, for the future **5** responsibility, take as much advantage as possible **6** felt differently, attending school **7** change from, normal school life **8** had not expected, do an exchange **9** mixed feelings, type of school **10** change, opinion of people

Extension idea Remind students that the ideas in the questions will probably not be expressed in the text using the same words. In fact, they should be careful when they do see the same words in the text as in the questions to check that the meaning is the same: 'word spotting' is a frequent reason why weaker students lose marks in this section. To sensitise them to this, ask students to paraphrase each question without reading the text (if necessary, ask them to cover the text).

You can get them started by giving 1 as an example: *didn't expect the education system to be so different.*

Elicit a paraphrase for 2 from the whole class, e.g. *liked helping the people I lived with.*

(Suggested paraphrases: **3** thought the experience has helped them to grow up. **4** thinks the experience has taught them useful skills. **5** considered they should make the most of the experience. **6** had a different attitude to going to school while they were on the exchange. **7** needed to get away from their normal school routine. **8** thought an exchange would be impossible. **9** liked some aspects of their new school, but were not so keen on others. **10** thought differently about people after the experience.)

3 ***Alternative treatment*** Ask students to work in pairs to find the answers and make the reading exercise a race to see which pair can find all the correct answers first.

Answers
1 D **2** C **3** C **4** A **5** B **6** C **7** A **8** A **9** D

Extension idea Ask students to discuss these questions:

- *Which of the exchange students do you think had the best experience?*
- *Which of the countries mentioned would interest you most for an educational exchange?*
- *Do the students mention anything you would definitely not like or enjoy?*

4 ***Extension idea*** When students have finished, ask one person from each group to present their ideas to the rest of the class.

Reading and Use of English | Part 3

1 EP ***As a warmer*** Write *culture shock* on the board and ask students what they think it means. (Answer: *A feeling of confusion felt by someone visiting a country or place that they do not know*)

Ask students in small groups:

- *Have you ever experienced culture shock? When, where, why?*
- *What do visitors to your country find confusing when they first arrive?*
- *What sort of things might cause culture shock for international students?*

Answers
2 intention **3** response (responsibility)
4 adjustment **5** comparison **6** existence
7 demand **8** development **9** behaviour
10 advice/advisor **11** appearance **12** knowledge

Alternative treatment Ask students to use their dictionaries to check their answers. They should also check carefully that they have spelled their answers correctly.

2

Answers
2 assess **3** feel **4** involve **5** investigate
6 confuse **7** prefer **8** approve

Extension idea Ask students what suffixes they can add to verbs to change them into nouns (looking at Exercises 1 and 2). (Answers: *-ment, -ing, -tion, -ation, -ence* (*-ent* changes to *-ence*), *-iour, -ledge*, and *-ise* sometimes changes to *-ice*.)

Ask students to brainstorm other words that change in these ways.

3 EP Point out to students that in the example, a plural noun is required.

Elicit that they need to check if they need a plural, a past tense form of a verb, a negative prefix, etc.

When they have finished, ask them to read through the completed text to make sure it makes sense.

They should then compare their answers in pairs and check in a dictionary cases where they are not sure of the correct spelling.

Answers
1 friendships **2** variety **3** expectations
4 comparison **5** unprepared **6** independent
7 behaviour **8** welcoming

4 When students have finished, round up with the whole class. These are some of the ideas which should come up in discussion: *Home students learn from meeting overseas students, especially tolerance, differences in cultures, differences in educational culture, how to be good hosts, how to show and share the things in their area/region. Hosting exchange students opens the opportunity for the school's own students to do similar exchanges abroad,* etc.

Extension idea Ask your students if they think having studied one language helps when learning another, e.g. there may be skills you learn which are transferable. You can turn this into a general discussion.

Speaking | Part 1

As a warmer Elicit what happens in Speaking Part 1 (this was covered in the Unit 1 Exam information box on page 15 of the Student's Book).

Alternative treatment With books closed, write these questions on the board and ask students to ask and answer them in pairs:

- *What is/was your favourite subject at school?*
- *How do you think you'll use English in the future?*

1 ▶ With books open, ask students to compare their answers with Nikolai's and Martyna's.

Answers
1 because 2 if 3 when (if) 4 who 5 if 6 and

CD 1 Track 17

See page 59 of the Student's Book.

2 Point out to students that both Nikolai and Martyna gain marks because they don't confine themselves to shortish, simple answers, they volunteer ideas and information and they sound enthusiastic.

Suggested answers
1 three
2 three
3 Candidates receive marks based on their ability to manage grammar and longer units of discourse. Candidates also achieve a higher score for longer, more complex sentences.
4 It creates a good, positive impression.

3 If you did the alternative treatment in the warmer, ask students to change partners to answer these questions again. Give students a little time to think before they start.

Extension idea If you did the alternative treatment in the warmer, round up by asking students to say how their answers were different the second time.

4 **Pronunciation:** word stress (2)

1 ▶ Tell students that stress does not always change. However:
- knowing how stress changes is an essential part of managing word formation
- getting stress right will help listeners to hear clearly which word you are using.

Ask students: *Which word* – necessary *or* necessity – *is a noun* (Answer: necessity), *and which an adjective* (Answer: necessary)?

Remind students how stress is shown in dictionaries:

Answers
necessary vs *necessity*.

CD 1 Track 18

I think English is really necessary.

I think English is an absolute necessity.

2 **Answers**
satisfying, satisfactory, educate, education, exam, examination, explain, explanation, graduate, graduation, possible, possibility, prefer, preference, refer, reference, relative, relation, institute, institution

Extension idea Ask students to check some of the answers in their dictionaries, so they can see how the dictionary can help them with pronunciation.

Point out that most good learner's dictionaries also come with a CD-ROM, so when students look up a word, they can also listen to it and repeat the pronunciation.

3 ▶

Answers
The stress is always on the syllable before the suffix (*-tion, -ity*).

CD 1 Track 19

See answers for Pronunciation Exercise 2.

4 ***Alternative treatment*** Ask students to take turns to test each other's pronunciation. One student points at a word on the list in Pronunciation Exercise 2 and the other has to say it aloud. The first student has to listen and correct the pronunciation if it's wrong.

5 Give students a minute or two to think how they will answer the questions. Tell them to also refer to Nikolai's and Martyna's answers in Exercise 1 to give more complete answers.

6 Tell students to correct their partners after they have finished speaking, and remind them not to interrupt.

7 Remind students that some questions may be somewhat predictable in Speaking Part 1, so they should think about how they would answer them before going to the exam. However, their answers should be spontaneous, not memorised, otherwise the examiner will be unable to give them a mark.

Extension idea Ask each pair of students to give each other feedback on how they performed. The criteria for feedback can be the points in Exercise 2.

Note: In Speaking Part 1, students may be asked a wide variety of questions about themselves, not just about their studies as practised here.

Writing | Part 1 An essay

1 ***As a warmer*** Ask students:

- *Which of the subjects you study at school do you think are most useful?* (If your students are no longer at school, ask the question in the past tense.)
- *How much freedom should young people have to decide what subjects they study at school?*

Alternative treatment Ask students to underline the key points in the task, then think about and note down some ideas before they discuss.

2 Remind students that they should organise their plans into paragraphs and that each paragraph should have a clearly different topic.

3

Suggested answers
1 No, because it's better to use your own words in the answer than repeat words from the task.
3 Yes. Candidates will lose marks if they don't cover all the points in the task, as they have not answered the question completely.

Extension idea Ask students in pairs: *How is Marina's plan different from yours? Which do you prefer? Why?*

4 Tell students to look carefully at the writing task again while they answer the questions. Remind them that they will be assessed for all the content being relevant to the task.

If you wish, ask students to cover Exercise 5 while they do this exercise.

5 Go through the teachers' comments carefully with students, pointing out the need for relevance and a clear statement of opinion.

Remind them that they will lose marks for irrelevance, lack of planning, poor organisation and not stating their opinion clearly.

Tell them their first paragraph should be quite short, so that they have plenty of space in the body of the essay to deal with the task adequately.

Answers
a 3 **b** 2 **c** 1

6 Ask students to base their paragraph on their opinions and the plan they wrote in Exercise 2, but using paragraph 3 in Exercise 4 as a model. Give them five minutes to write the paragraph.

When they have finished, they should compare paragraphs in small groups.

Round up by asking a few students to read out what they have written to the whole class and discuss or comment on the paragraphs as necessary.

If you wish, ask students to rewrite their paragraphs, putting comments into practice.

7

Answers
1 with the result that **2** Also **3** for example when **4** These opportunities **5** if **6** A further point is that **7** It **8** For all these reasons **9** do so

Extension idea When students have finished, go through the answers with them, eliciting the function of each word/phrase in the context to show them how these linking words and phrases help to add coherence to the answer. (Suggested answers: **1** The phrase links the need to communicate in English with the fact that many jobs are international. **2** It adds another point. **3** It introduces an example into the sentence. **4** *These opportunities* relates the final sentence to *work in different countries* and *their companies send them abroad.* **5** *If* relates speaking the local language to enjoying holidays and learning about places. **6** The phrase introduces a new paragraph with a new topic. **7** *It* relates the second sentence of the paragraph to *the Internet* in the first sentence. **8** As an opening phrase in the concluding paragraph, *For all these reasons* brings all the previously stated reasons together without having to repeat them. **9** *Do so* avoids repeating *learn a foreign language.*)

8 Give students up to ten minutes for this exercise.

9 Encourage students to use linking phrases from Exercise 7 in their answers.

Sample answer

In the modern world, it is essential for young people to get experience of other countries and other cultures, not only to learn the language, but also to learn to live with people from other parts of the world. For this reason, I believe it is a good idea to do an international exchange.

Young people who study abroad have to study in the language of the country they visit, with the result that they gain extra language skills. They also learn to interact with people from other countries and understand their interests and way of life.

Another major advantage of studying abroad is that young people learn independence, because many of them live away from home for the first time. This allows them to return home more mature and self-confident than they were when they left.

Finally, I think it is important to build international understanding, and this can be achieved when young people form friendships across borders.

For all these reasons, I am strongly in favour of giving people the chance to study abroad when they are young.

6 My first job

Unit objectives

- **Reading and Use of English Part 5:** scanning the text; training in understanding the text before reading the multiple-choice options
- **Reading and Use of English Part 2:** reviewing language work done previously in the unit
- **Writing Part 2:** writing a letter or an email; analysing the task; brainstorming ideas; planning; spelling and frequent spelling mistakes
- **Listening Part 3:** listening for gist; identifying key ideas in questions
- **Speaking Part 2:** phrases for expressing similarities and making comparisons
- **Pronunciation:** sentence stress (2)
- **Vocabulary:** confusion between *work* and *job*; *possibility, occasion* and *opportunity*; *fun* and *funny*; collocations with *job* and *work*; lexis to describe jobs: *involve, deal with,* etc.
- **Grammar:** countable and uncountable nouns; using *piece, bit, deal, amount* and *number* with countable and uncountable nouns; definite and indefinite articles; zero article

Starting off

As a warmer Before students open their books, either with the whole class or in groups, ask students:

- *What jobs do teenagers typically do to earn extra money?*
- *What jobs do you do?*
- *Have you heard of any unusual jobs done by students?*

Students then answer the questions in Starting off.

Extension idea Ask:

- *In which of these jobs would it be useful to speak English?*
- *What do students gain or learn from doing jobs like these? Is it just money, or is there something else?*

Listening | Part 3

1 **Suggested answers**
B I didn't expect to have to work so hard **C** I get a lot of new ideas from the people I meet **D** I might get the chance to do something I've always wanted to **E** I'm learning to do new things **F** not all the job is fun, but some of it is **G** I like not having to rely on my parents for money **H** I get annoyed when there are problems I can't solve

Extension idea Ask students in small groups to paraphrase each of the alternatives by saying: *How do you think the speakers might express each of these feelings or opinions when you listen?* (Suggested answers: **A** I get the impression that people like talking to me. **B** It's more tiring than I expected. **C** You find out things from the people you talk to. **D** I might be able to fulfill one of my dreams. **E** I'm learning things which I'll be able to use in future. **F** It's not all fun – some things are better than others. **G** It's great to have my own money to spend. **H** I wish I could solve all the problems.)

2 Before listening, tell students to:

- listen to the whole of each piece before choosing an answer
- be cautious about choosing an answer where they have heard the speaker using some of the same words. 'Word spotting' is often the sign of a weaker student; they should be listening for the same meaning to be expressed, probably using different words.

When they have listened twice, give students time to check and compare their answers in pairs. Ask them to try to quote, approximately, the words which gave them the answers.

Answers
1 A **2** E **3** B **4** H **5** D

CD 1 Track 20

Speaker 1: This is my first student job and I'm a part-time hospital porter taking patients to different departments for treatment. It's hard physical work, but I think I expected that when I started.

For me, the best thing's the human contact with, you know, older people who've had interesting lives – well, actually everyone's older than me, I'm only 18. I hear lots of good stories, and [1]they have the opportunity to talk about things outside the hospital, which probably makes them feel better and brightens up their stay a bit. At least, I think it does.

Speaker 2: I'm just 17 and I'm working as a trainee receptionist in a hotel. I'm normally quite shy really, but I'm really happy to be doing this job because it's great to be getting some work experience. Anyway, they've given me lots of responsibility quite early on, so [2]I've learned to do all the sorts of things which you need for almost any job, really practical things like how to answer the phone correctly – you know, not just saying 'Hey' or whatever. On some occasions, I've also been left on my own in charge of the whole hotel. That's really built up my self-confidence.

Speaker 3: Well, [3]nobody expects babysitting to be a complete doddle, at least not when there are three small kids to look after. But, well, their mum's very nice and she did warn me – and she's paying me over the usual rate because she knows what it's like – she has to have them when I'm not around – but [3]I really think I've let myself in for a lot more than I bargained for. I've done babysitting before, but it's never been like this. They never stop running around and shouting, and bath time – well, that's just chaos. I reckon I get wetter than they do!

Speaker 4: It isn't a very well-paid job and it's not exactly fun, but then first jobs usually aren't. But I'm earning my own money for the first time – not enough to live on, but it's a start. I'm working in a call centre for a large computer company, answering customers' queries, complaints, um, you know, whatever. Sometimes they just want information, but often it's a real problem which I have to help them sort out. Sometimes it's quite simple and that's fine because with a few instructions they go away happy, but I don't have any training in computer skills, [4]so often I can't help them and I hate that.

Speaker 5: Well, I'm only making the tea and coffee and running round doing odd jobs – I'm a typical runner on a film set, basically. It sounds terribly glamorous, doesn't it? But the money's not great – actually, I reckon it costs more in train tickets than I actually earn, but what an experience! I'm getting to see exactly how films are made, and the people are really funny, so there are lots of laughs on set – though I do have to keep quiet and only speak when spoken to. [5]There's even the possibility that I'll be given a small part, and that, well, that'd be a dream come true!

Extension idea Print out and photocopy the recording script from the Teacher's Resources CD-ROM and the word list for this unit. Ask students to:

- underline the words/phrases which give the correct answers. You can play the recording again for them to follow while they are doing this
- find these phrases (which you will need to write on the board) in the script: *brighten up, build up, a complete doddle, over the usual rate, I've let myself in for a lot more than I bargained for, not enough to live on, sort out, odd jobs, a dream come true.*

In pairs, ask students to discuss what each phrase means in the context. Then ask students to check their ideas in the word list or in the dictionary.

3 ***Alternative treatment*** Play 'What's my job?'. Students take turns to think of a job and mime one action they would have to do in this job. Other members of the group then ask questions to find out what the job is. The student who is being questioned can only answer 'Yes' or 'No'.

Vocabulary

work or *job*; *possibility*, *occasion* or *opportunity*; *fun* or *funny*

1 ***Alternative treatment*** Ask students to read the definitions before they do the exercise. If you wish, you can play Track 20 again for students to check.

Answers
1 job **2** work **3** opportunity **4** occasions
5 job; jobs **6** funny **7** possibility

2

Answers
1 funny **2** fun **3** possibility **4** occasions
5 opportunity **6** job **7** work **8** jobs

Extension idea Ask students to write four sentences of their own illustrating some of these words. Ask them to leave the word itself blank. They then pass their sentences to another student who must write the correct word in the gap.

3 If you have photocopied the word list, students can use this to help them do some of the exercise.

Suggested answers
2 badly paid **4** challenging **5** demanding
6 tiring **7** tough **9** office **11** manual **13** holiday
14 part-time **15** permanent **16** temporary
17 weekend **19** pleasant **20** responsible
21 worthwhile

4 ***Extension idea*** Ask students to each think of two other jobs (not on the list) and how they can describe them.

Then, in small groups, they take turns to describe their job. The other students must guess what jobs they are describing and, if necessary, ask questions to find out more.

Reading and Use of English | Part 5

Background information Lucy Irvine has written several books, including *Castaway*, her account of a year she spent on a desert island, also made into a film, and *Runaway*, the first part of her autobiography.

1 ***Extension idea*** In some countries, it is more usual to work for your parents than in others. You can develop the discussion by asking some of these questions, as appropriate:

- *Would you like to work with your parents? Would it be easier or more difficult than working for another employer?*
- *Do you think young people who work with their parents should go directly into the family business, or should they get experience elsewhere?*
- *Should they be treated the same or differently from other workers?*
- *Do you think young people have a duty to work with their parents if they are asked to?*

2 Give students three minutes to do this.

Answers
1 She was a waitress.
2 The special role her dad created for her, creating packed lunches, cakes and puddings

3 These questions are nearly the same as the stems of the multiple-choice questions in Exercise 4. The intention is to encourage students to find the part of the text which answers the questions *before* looking at the options A–D. Students are often confused by looking at the options first and then reading the text to find the correct answer. In most cases, better results are obtained by understanding the text first, then finding the option which corresponds, and this is the procedure recommended in the Teacher's Handbook for the exam.

Suggested underlining
1 None of us had ever worked in a hotel before.
2 impressive chef's hat and a terrifying ability to lose his temper and get violent
3 I … always grabbed the dishes he set down with a forbidding expression on my face which was transformed into a charming smile in the brief space between kitchen and dining room.
4 and I took pleasure in my ability to get on with the people at each table. It was funny how differently people behaved in the evenings, dressed up and talking with louder, colder voices, not always returning my smile.
5 the most extraordinary collection of puddings, cakes and other desserts ever to grace a Scottish hotel. Most were things I had invented myself and I had cooked all of them. Some – Jacobite Grenades, Mocha Genghis Khan and Goat's Milk Bavarios to name a few – were undeniably strange.

4 Point out that these are the same questions as in Exercise 3 (with the exception of question 6, which refers to the whole text). Tell students to read what they have underlined for Exercise 3, then look at the options to find the one which coincides.

Answers
1 C 2 B 3 D 4 B 5 D 6 B

Extension idea Ask students to work in small groups.

Tell them to underline unfamiliar vocabulary in the text and then ask each other in their groups if they can explain any of the vocabulary they have underlined.

Tell them to choose a maximum of three items of vocabulary they would like to have explained (this will encourage them to discriminate between working on more or less useful vocabulary – if they are not sure how to choose, tell them to choose vocabulary which prevents them understanding part of the text).

Write the words each group has chosen on the board. Then ask each group to guess the meanings from the context.

If you wish to make it competitive, tell them that the group which guesses the most correct meanings is the winner.

As a follow-up, students can check by using the word list or their dictionaries.

5 You can also ask students if it is easy for teenagers to find holiday jobs in their country, or whether it is better to travel abroad.

Speaking | Part 2

As a warmer To start a whole-class discussion, ask students: *Do you think the most important thing about a job is the money you earn? Why? / Why not? What other things are important?*

1 With books open, point out to students that if they also look for similarities between the ideas illustrated by the two photos, they may find more to say.

2 Remind students that they should aim to use a range of appropriate vocabulary when speaking and to use language they have learned recently, not just language they feel comfortable with.

> **Answers**
> See recording script for Track 21.

Extension idea Ask students to look back through the unit and see if there is other vocabulary they could use to talk about these photos. They can also look at the word list if it has been photocopied.

Alternative treatment If students have access to the recording script, they can do Exercises 3, 4 and 5 while reading and listening. (You can print out and photocopy the script from the Teacher's Resources CD-ROM.)

3 

> **Answers**
> **a** B **b** B **c** B **d** 2 **e** 1 **f** 2 **g** 2 **h** 1 **i** 2

CD 1 Track 21

Examiner: Here are your photographs. They show young people doing jobs. I'd like you to compare the photographs and say what you think the people are learning from doing these two types of work.

Nikolai: Well, OK, so firstly I can say that both photos show young people, perhaps teenagers, working. Er, both the jobs in the photos involve working in situations where they need good skills in dealing with people in the correct way. I'm sure neither of them is very well paid. Anyway, the first photo shows a girl serving young people in a restaurant, whereas in the second photo a boy is working with children and coaching them to play football. The girl's job may be full time, whereas the boy's is probably part time. I think both can learn a lot from these jobs. The girl can learn how to keep customers happy, while the boy has to keep children in order. The girl has to learn to work efficiently under pressure. On the other hand, the boy has to learn to keep cool. He'll probably learn not just to deal with children, but also their parents.

Examiner: Thank you. Antonia, which of these jobs would you prefer to do?

Antonia: I'd prefer to coach children than work in a restaurant because really I enjoy being in the fresh air more than being indoors. And I like kids.

Examiner: Thank you.

4

> **Answer**
> b

Extension idea You can refer students back to the way Martyna did the task in Unit 2 by talking about one photo for some time and then the other. You may also play the recording from Unit 2 (CD 1 Track 07) to contrast the two approaches.

Tell students that both approaches are good and that they are both strategies that are worth practising for the exam.

5

> **Answers**
> See recording script for Track 21 (Nikolai does not use the phrases *While the girl in the first photo … , Another thing in the second photo is …*)

Extension idea Ask students: *Which phrases can be used to express similarities?* (Answers: Both photos show, Both the jobs in the photos involve, neither of them, I think both can, Not just … but also)

6 Pronunciation: sentence stress (2)

As a warmer Ask students: *What do you remember about sentence stress from Unit 2? Which words do we normally stress in a sentence?* (Answer: Words which carry the most meaning, usually nouns, verbs and adjectives) Ask students to look back at page 25 to remind themselves.

1 and 2

> **Answers**
> **1** first, girl, young people, restaurant, second, boy, children
> **2** Anyway, the first photo shows a girl serving young people in a restaurant, whereas in the second photo, a boy is working with children.

CD 1 Track 22

See page 66 of the Student's Book.

3 

Answers
The girl's job may be full time, whereas the boy's is probably part time.
The girl can learn how to keep customers happy, while the boy has to keep children in order.
He'll probably learn not just to deal with children, but also their parents.
I'd prefer to coach children than work in a restaurant because really I enjoy being in the fresh air more than being indoors.

CD 1 Track 23

See Answers above.

4 ***Extension idea*** When students have finished, ask one student in each pair to close their books. The other student in the pair should read out the first half of the sentence while the first student should complete it from memory and with the correct contrastive stress. If the student cannot remember how to complete the sentence, the first student should complete it for them by reading.

They can then change roles and do the exercise again.

7 Tell students to listen to their partners and correct anything they do not agree with.

8 and 9 Give students a little time to prepare. Student A should look back over this section. Student B might benefit by looking at vocabulary describing feelings from Unit 2, either in the book or on the word list.

Alternative treatment Elicit a checklist from the class, which you can write on the board, of things students/candidates should aim to do. Here are some suggestions:

- talk equally about both photos
- mention similarities as well as differences
- talk about the photos in general rather than describe small details
- concentrate on answering the examiner's question (printed with the photos)
- keep speaking for a minute
- try to use language and vocabulary you have studied recently.

Ask the student who is listening to use the checklist to give feedback and advice to their partner when they have finished.

Round up feedback ideas with the whole class.

Grammar

Countable and uncountable nouns

As a warmer Write on the board:

- *He's had three jobs since he left school.*
- *I'm going to give you two advices.*

Ask which sentence is correct, and ask students to correct the other. (Answer: I'm going to give you some advice / two pieces of advice.) Ask which noun you can count: *advice* or *jobs*. (Answer: jobs)

Point out that all nouns in English are either countable or uncountable. Then move on to the exercises in the book.

1 You can also point out that the most common mistake candidates make with countable and uncountable nouns is to make uncountable nouns countable.

When students have done the exercise, go through the notes in the Language reference section on page 165 (Countable and uncountable nouns) with them. If your students have the concept of countable/uncountable nouns in their own language(s), point out that nouns that are countable in their language may be uncountable in English and vice versa. You could invite them to give examples (e.g. in Spanish *muebles* and *consejos* are countable, while in English *furniture* and *advice* are uncountable).

Point out that *news* is uncountable although it ends in 's', and is therefore grammatically singular. You can also elicit ways of expressing the uncountable nouns in a countable form, e.g. *an item of news, a piece of news*.

Answers
1 ~~informations~~ information **2** ~~an advice~~ some / a piece of / a bit of advice **3** ~~a work~~ work / a job
4 correct **5** ~~accommodations~~ accommodation
6 correct **7** ~~furnitures~~ furniture **8** ~~many damages~~ much damage **9** ~~luggages~~ luggage
10 ~~musics~~ music

2

Answers
Students should circle: **2** advice; information; knowledge; news **3** damage; transport **4** furniture **5** food **6** homework; work **7** equipment **8** music

3

Answers
1 piece/bit **2** number **3** piece/bit **4** piece/bit **5** deal **6** number; amount

This would be a suitable moment to do the photocopiable activity on the Teacher's Resources CD-ROM.

Articles

4 When students have finished, go through the Language reference on page 163 with them. Ask them to suggest other examples for each rule as you go through them.

Answers
2 c 3 f 4 d 5 e 6 a

5

Answers
1 the **2** an **3** the **4** – **5** a **6** a **7** – **8** the **9** the **10** – **11** the **12** a

6 Tell students to pay careful attention to articles when they are writing and speaking, and to correct mistakes when they notice them.

Answers
1 ~~a latest news~~ the latest news **2** ~~my age~~ the age **3** town ~~the~~ next year **4** useful information on *the* internet **5** parking in *the* city centre **6** are *the* most effective **7** ~~The money~~ Money **8** listening to ~~the~~ music **9** ~~the~~ foreign cities; ~~the~~ shopping **10** having *a* wonderful time **11** ~~a~~ plenty of spare time at ~~this~~ *the* moment; have ~~a~~ dinner **12** ~~an~~ accommodation

Extension idea Collect examples of mistakes your students have made with articles in their own recent written work and ask them to find and correct them.

Reading and Use of English | Part 2

As a warmer With books closed, write these phrases on the board:

- *Summer arts or music school*
- *Outdoors activities course*
- *Community work*
- *Summer job*
- *Language course*

Ask students: *Which of these things have you done in your summer holidays? Which did you enjoy most? Why?*

Get students to recount their experiences in small groups.

Tell students: *Imagine your school or college is thinking of organising activities for its students for a few weeks during the summer holidays. Discuss how each of these activities can benefit young people and decide which* ***two*** *activities the school should organise.*

1 With books open, give students a minute to skim the article.

Answers
rock climbing, rafting, trekking, designing and implementing a volunteering project

2 Remind students that they should think what type of word they need for each gap, the meaning of the whole sentence, and whether the word forms part of a fixed phrase.

To illustrate the last point, elicit the meaning of the example *take part in* (Answer: participate).

Remind students that they should read the whole sentence before deciding what word will fit the gap – question 1 is an example of the need to do this.

Ask them to work alone at first, then to compare their answers in pairs.

Answers
1 get **2** If **3** the **4** every **5** So **6** away **7** such **8** just/only

3 When they have finished, tell students to read through the whole text to check that it makes sense.

4 ***Alternative treatment*** If you wish, make this a whole-class discussion.

Writing | Part 2 A letter or email

1 ***As a warmer*** Ask students in groups: *Do you have friends or people you know who you write to in English using, for example, email or Facebook? How do you know these people? What do you write about? How often do you correspond?*

Alternative treatment With books open, ask students: *Do you ever use email or Facebook to help with homework? Are these good ways of working together? What are the advantages?*

Suggested underlining
jobs students do, describing, in your country, problems, best way to find a good student job

2 If your students are from different countries, they can do this exercise by telling each other about what happens in their country and comparing the two.

3 ***Extension idea*** Ask students to change partners and compare their plans. Afterwards, give them a little time to make changes to their plans if they wish.

4 Tell students that if they are not sure how to begin a paragraph (a problem many students have), they can start by saying what the paragraph is about; they can then fill in the details in the rest of the paragraph.

Alternative treatment Ask students in pairs to read the email and say how Pablo's plan is similar to and how it is different from theirs.

If your students are Spanish, or you have some Spanish students in class, ask them: *Do you agree with what Pablo says about students' jobs in Spain?*

If your students are from other countries, ask them: *How is the situation similar and how is it different in this/your country?*

Answers
1 *It's good* … indicates that he is answering the email + being friendly; *I hope* … rounds off the email in a friendly way. In the exam, both these sentences will make the email sound more authentic.
2 The first sentence of the paragraphs tells us the subject of the paragraph.

Extension idea Elicit other ways of beginning letters and emails. (Suggested answer: *Dear/Hello* + name)

Elicit other ways of ending letters and emails. (Suggested answers: *Yours, Best wishes, Kind regards, Yours sincerely,* etc.)

5 Tell students that spelling mistakes are the most frequent type of mistake made by candidates. Correct spelling is important, as mistakes create a bad impression on the examiner and can sometimes make writing difficult to understand. The mistakes in this email and in Exercise 6 are among the most frequent, and it is worth paying attention and learning how to spell these words correctly.

Answers
~~restaurans~~ restaurants; ~~easely~~ easily; ~~studing~~ studying; ~~wich~~ which; ~~payed~~ paid; ~~usefull~~ useful; ~~becaus~~ because; ~~corses~~ courses; ~~especialy~~ especially; ~~advertisment~~ advertisement

6 EP Ask students to check their answers by looking at the Language reference section on page 176 (The most common spelling errors by candidates).

Answers
The spelling of these words should be corrected as follows:
embarrassing, opportunity, comfortable, grateful, environment, necessary, beginning, communicate, excellent, forward, prefer, received, recommend, which

7 Ask students to work alone to do this exercise. Once they have finished, they should work in pairs and compare their ideas.

Suggested underlining
first jobs, describing your first job, someone you know well, when, what, learned, any problems

8 This writing task is probably best done for homework.

Sample answer
Hi Bob,
It's nice to hear from you again.
My first job, which I did for a month during my last summer holidays, was as a part-time assistant at a shoe shop in my town. I used to work every day from 9 a.m. until lunchtime serving customers. Basically, I had to welcome them to the shop and help them to find the shoes they were looking for.
The job was a good experience because I learned how to deal with customers and help them to make up their minds when they were not sure what they wanted. On days when there weren't many customers, I had to tidy the store room, which was quite boring, but I certainly also learned a lot about shoes: which are comfortable, what sort of shoes suit different types of people and so on.
I didn't have any particular difficulties except when dealing with customers who were rude or in too much of a hurry, but I managed to smile just the same.
Good luck with your project!
Louise

Extension idea Give students a deadline for doing the writing task.

When they bring their emails to class, ask them to exchange them with a partner. Their partner should read the email using this checklist (which you can write on the board):

- *Does the email deal with all parts of the task?*
- *Is it divided into paragraphs, and does each paragraph deal with a separate part of the task?*
- *Are the articles (a, an, the) used correctly?*
- *Are there any spelling mistakes?*

When students have finished reading, they should give their partners feedback. Then give students five or ten minutes as necessary to make any changes before they hand in their answers to you.

Vocabulary and grammar review Unit 5

1 **1** get away with **2** put off; got over **3** live up to **4** look back; turned out **5** handed back; pointed out

2 **1** learn **2** study **3** teaching **4** join; get to know **5** attend **6** take part

3 **1** harder, he would / he'd **2** study abroad, you will become / you'll become **3** she would not / wouldn't attend **4** look after my book **5** knew the answer, I would **6** he wasn't / was not so tired

4 **1** preference **2** knowledge **3** behaviour **4** comparison **5** activities **6** assistance **7** measurement **8** ability

Vocabulary and grammar review Unit 6

1 **1** occasion **2** work **3** job **4** occasion **5** fun **6** opportunity **7** funny **8** possibility

2 **1** had such / so much / a lot of fun on **2** have/get/take the/an opportunity to speak **3** have the possibility of studying **4** was much better than **5** with a good/great deal of **6** on one occasion

3 **1** deal **2** bit/piece **3** bit/piece **4** bit/piece **5** number

4 **1** – **2** a **3** the **4** a **5** – **6** a **7** – **8** a **9** the **10** a **11** a **12** – **13** a **14** an **15** the **16** an **17** –

7 High adventure

Unit objectives

- **Reading and Use of English Part 6:** understanding the structure and organisation of the text; using cohesive features and reference devices
- **Reading and Use of English Part 4:** how to approach the task; avoiding common problems
- **Writing Part 2:** writing an article
- **Listening Part 2:** identifying what information is required
- **Listening Part 4:** identifying the main idea in the questions; listening for gist and detail
- **Speaking Part 3:** suggesting ideas; asking opinion; agreeing and disagreeing; involving your partner and reacting to their ideas
- **Pronunciation:** intonation (2)
- **Vocabulary:** sports and adventure sports; verb collocations with sporting activities: *do sport*, etc.; *look*, *see*, *watch*, *listen* and *hear*; words connected with sport
- **Grammar:** infinitive and verb + *-ing* forms

Starting off

1 ***As a warmer*** With books closed, ask students in small groups: *Can you name any adventure sports, for example, parachuting?*

If you wish, make it a competition to see which group can name the largest number of adventure sports in, say, two minutes. (Possible answers: skiing, hiking, mountaineering, snowboarding, abseiling, bungee jumping, hot-air ballooning, heli-skiing, tobogganing, tombstoning, zorbing, scuba diving + those in Starting off)

Students then do the exercise in the book.

Answers
1 mountain biking **2** rock climbing
3 snowboarding **4** windsurfing **5** canoeing/kayaking **6** parasailing/parascending

2 When students have finished, round up question 2 by asking them to tell the rest of the class about their experiences. Encourage the class to ask questions.

Listening | Part 2

1 ***As a warmer*** Tell students they are going to read and hear about a very hard type of race. Ask them to brainstorm types of races which are very hard, long or dangerous (e.g. marathons, round-the-world yacht races, Tour de France cycle race, the 152-mile Spartathlon) and ask why they think people do these races.

Elicit that when students listen to complete the notes, they will need between one and three words for each answer.

Suggest they also think about the type of words they might need (noun, adjective, etc.) and look at other clues, e.g. in question 1 *his* tells them they need a noun/noun phrase.

Suggested answers
1 a person or group of people **2** a time or place **3** a type of person **4** a type of person **5** a type of (probably natural) place **6** people, place or thing **7** a title **8** a time (duration) **9** a type of ability or activity **10** a descriptive adjective / an opinion

2 ▶ After students have listened twice, give them some time to complete their answers and check their spelling. They can then compare their answers in pairs.

Answers
1 family **2** (early) 1990s **3** men and women / women and men **4** specialists **5** mountains or deserts / deserts or mountains **6** inhabitants
7 South Island **8** ten/10 days **9** staying awake
10 (very) motivating

Extension idea Print out and photocopy the recording script from the Teacher's Resources CD-ROM. Play the recording a third time, while students follow the script to check their answers.

CD 1 Track 24

Gary: ... so I'm going to talk to you about adventure racing as my part of the project. Adventure racing's a sport you do in teams, and I got interested in this because I actually took part in one for the first time last year in the north of England with the rest of my [1]family, and we were racing against lots of other teams made up of people of different ages. Anyway, I've done some research and what I've found out turns out to be much more interesting than I expected. The sport's been around for some time. There were races as far back as a hundred years ago and some newish ones which were started in the 1970s and 80s, but really people have been doing adventure racing in large numbers since the [2]early 1990s, and it's one of the toughest sports you can imagine. Unlike marathons or pentathlons or those sorts of things, where the winner's the individual runner who finishes first, in adventure races the winners are the first team of four to six people, depending on the race, to all get over the finishing line together, and in many races one of the rules is that the team must be made up of an equal number of [3]men and women – two or three of each depending on the size of the team. Anyway, it's not like just going jogging or running or something like that. These races combine a mixture of different activities or sports – running, swimming, kayaking, climbing and cycling to name just some of them. I've been looking a bit at the teams who win, and one of the things I've noticed is that the winning teams tend to contain [4]specialists in different skills, such as climbing and kayaking, and that seems to give them an advantage. The races are organised in all sorts of different places. Occasionally, they're organised in cities – there's a very famous one which takes place in Chicago – you know, in North America – but the majority are held in [5]mountains or deserts. This apparently heightens the sense of adventure and actually makes the race more hazardous because the course runs over an area which has little in the way of roads, certainly no telephones or hotels, and probably very few [6]inhabitants, so competitors are really isolated and on their own. Of course, they do carry a radio so they can call for help if they run into real trouble. Well, perhaps it won't surprise you, but I want to do more of these races, and one of the goals I've set myself is to go to New Zealand and do one of the most spectacular races in the world, the [7]South Island Race, where you run, cycle and kayak for 160 miles through mountains and down rivers. If that race sounds hard to you, and I guess it is, remember it only takes about 24 hours to do the whole course. I say 'only' because some of them go on for as long as [8]ten days. Now that's really extreme. At the moment, I'd say that two or three days would be my absolute maximum interms of endurance. Competitors have to carry everything they need with them – clothes, food and drink, the lot – and if they run out, they just go hungry or thirsty. On long races, my impression is that the greatest problem is just [9]staying awake, because there are no fixed times for breaks, so teams tend to go on racing for as many hours as they can. In fact, I've heard of people falling asleep while they're riding a bike and that, as you can imagine, can be really dangerous. Just to finish off, another interesting fact: many people who are at the top of their sport in other fields are now taking part because they find that, rather than competing as individuals as they've done all their lives in sports stadiums and the like, they need to work as a team and help each other, and they find this [10]very motivating. I think there's often quite a learning curve for other sports professionals.

3 To help students, you can ask:

- *What do you think happens when one member of the team is much slower or faster than the others?*
- *How can teams help members who are having problems?*
- *Do you think teams do better if all the members have the same skills or different skills?*

Vocabulary

Verb collocations with sporting activities

1 ***As a warmer*** With books closed, tell students that they have got to call out the correct verb to complete the sentences you say. You then say the sentences below. If students suggest the correct verb, indicate this with a thumbs up. If the wrong verb, with a thumbs down. If you notice that they are 'getting' the rules, carry on with sentences till they have got them.

- *I love to mmm jogging early in the morning.* (They should suggest 'go'.)
- *I mmm more sport at weekends than during the week.* (do)
- *I used to mmm basketball when I was a student.* (play)
- *I should mmm more exercise.* (do)
- *Martin likes to mmm cycling, especially in summer.* (go)
- *When I retire, I think I'll mmm golf every day.* (play)

With books open, students should answer the questions and then check their answers in the recording script if they have access to it.

Answers
1 do **2** going **3** organised **4** held **5** taking part; competing

2 ***Alternative treatment*** Ask students to study the table. Then tell them to work in pairs and add two or three more nouns to the lists for *go*, *play* and *do*.

If you wish, you can call out the activities below in a random order.

- *do karate, weightlifting, pilates*
- *play rugby, badminton, table tennis*
- *go running, sailing, walking*

Answers
1 organise/hold; compete / take part / enter
2 go; doing/taking **3** play; play; go

3 ***Extension idea*** Ask students to write a paragraph for homework answering one of the two questions.

Reading and Use of English | Part 6

When preparing to teach this section, decide if you wish to do the alternative treatment for Exercises 2 and 3, as it involves some photocopying and other preparation in advance.

1 Remind students that it is important to read the title and that if there are any illustrations with the text in the exam, to look at them too, as they will have been included to help candidates.

Suggested answer
The title and the subheading suggest that we are going to read about what adventure racing involves.

Extension idea Students have practised Reading and Use of English Part 6 in Units 1 and 4. Elicit the best procedure for dealing with this task type before they start:

- Read the gapped text carefully, making a note of the paragraph topics in the margin as they read.
- Underline cohesive and referencing devices in the sentences as they read them one by one and place them.

2 When students have finished, ask them to compare their answers with a partner.

Alternative treatment for Exercises 2 and 3 Before the lesson, make one photocopy of the text and the missing sentences for each student.

Cut each of the missing sentences A–G into strips and place all the A sentences in one pile, all the B sentences in another pile and so on.

In class, hand out the text only and do Exercise 2 as indicated in the Student's Book.

When you come to Exercise 3, ask students to work in pairs. Hand out just sentence A to each pair.

Tell them to read it, underline any cohesive or reference devices in it and decide which gap it will fill.

Once they have decided, round up the correct answer with the whole class and ask for reasons. (Answer: gap 6)

Repeat the process for sentence B, etc.

When they reach sentence D, they should identify that it is the distractor simply because it will not fit anywhere.

By following this process, you are showing students a way of working methodically through the missing sentences where they have:

- read the text carefully once
- dealt with the sentences one by one and seen that each of them can only fill one possible gap
- avoided reading back and forth between multiple missing sentences and gaps.

You can tell them that this is the quickest and most effective approach to this task, i.e. dealing with each sentence in order and one by one.

Suggested answers
Para. 2: type of team which is successful
Para. 3: Rebecca's first race
Para. 4: Training for Australia
Para. 5: How they started the race in Australia
Para. 6: their result in the race
Para. 7: conclusion

3 **Suggested underlining**
A Another, his feet **B** followed them **C** We won it even so, Eco-Challenge in Australia **D** His, it
E That (was how much I had prepared) **F** When I did it **G** To achieve this
1 G **2** F **3** C **4** E **5** B **6** A

Extension idea Remind students that they should quickly read through the completed text when they have finished to check their answers. Give them two minutes to do this.

4 You can also ask students if there is a sport they would really like to try.

Grammar

Infinitive and verb + *-ing*

1 Tell students that if they know these rules, they can avoid some of the frequent errors with infinitive and verb + *-ing* which candidates make at this level.

Ask them particularly to pay attention to the lists of verbs + infinitive and verb + verb + *-ing* in the Language reference section on page 166, as it is a good idea to memorise these verbs.

Answers
2 f **3** g **4** b, i **5** i **6** d **7** a **8** c **9** h **10** a

Extension idea Ask students to work in pairs and write one more example for each rule.

2 When checking the answers, ask students to say which rule each sentence is an example of.

Answers
1 starting **2** to go **3** to hold **4** Training
5 to get **6** injuring **7** running **8** pushing

3 **Answers**
1 to do **2** to learn **3** doing **4** taking part in

4 ***Extension idea*** Ask students to add two or three more questions of their own.

5 Tell students that mistakes using the infinitive and the verb + *-ing* form are very common in the exam. Encourage them to check which is correct using the notes in the Language reference section. Remind them that when they are doing homework, they can always check which is the correct form by referring to their dictionaries.

Answers
1 ~~running~~ to run **2** ~~spending~~ to spend
3 ~~to live~~ living **4** ~~to run~~ running **5** correct
6 ~~take~~ taking **7** ~~to win~~ in winning
8 ~~to sit and read~~ (with) sitting and reading
9 correct **10** ~~ride~~ riding / ~~for~~ to

This would be a suitable moment to do the photocopiable activity from the Teacher's Resources CD-ROM.

Reading and Use of English | Part 4

These questions practise use of the infinitive and verb + *-ing*. In the exam, a much wider range of grammar and lexical knowledge is tested.

1 These questions highlight common pitfalls which you can point out to students, i.e. using more than five words, changing the word given, not using the word given. You may want to remind students about the word limit before they start.

Answers
1 **A**: too many words
B: correct
C: *suggest* is not followed by the infinitive, and the option doesn't use the word given without changing it
D: doesn't use the word given
2 **A**: correct
B: too many words
C: changes the word given
D: doesn't use the word given

2 These questions show a step-by-step process to reach the correct answer.

Answers
1 (in order / so as) to get ready **2** could not / couldn't help laughing **3** are not allowed to use

3 and 4 Students should try to do these questions without using the clues in Exercise 4, and then use the clues to help them check whether their answers are correct.

Answers
1 taking part in **2** more expensive to hire
3 to give her a ring/call **4** succeeded in winning **5** to lose his temper with **6** had no difficulty (in) learning

Listening | Part 4

1 Paragliding is a sport where you jump from a high place, such as the top of a mountain or an aircraft, with a special parachute that allows you to fly a long distance before you land.

As a warmer Ask the class:

- *Have any of you ever done a risky sport? If so, what?*
- *Why do you think people do dangerous sports, for example, parachuting or climbing?*

2 To replicate the exam, give students 45 seconds to do this.

Suggested underlining
1 try paragliding **2** choose, in France
3 advantage of learning, sand dune **4** spend the first morning **5** started, instructor **6** when you land, it feels like **7** best reason

3 Remind students that they should pay attention to the interviewer's questions, as these will help them to follow the recording and indicate when they should be listening for the answer to the next question.

Answers
1 A 2 C 3 B 4 A 5 B 6 A 7 C

Extension idea Print and photocopy the recording script from the Teacher's Resources CD-ROM. Play the recording again and, as students follow the script, ask them to check their answers.

CD 1 Track 25

Interviewer: So, Hannah, what made you want to go on a paragliding course? It sounds like an extremely risky thing to want to do, even for a journalist like yourself.

Hannah: Well, I thought it was a bit risky too. I mean, as a sports journalist, I spend my life watching people do different sports and I've done a fair number of them myself. It's one of the qualifications for the job, I suppose. Anyway, a couple of years ago, I was actually in Switzerland playing golf with friends. I was researching for an article on golf courses and, you know, golf isn't the most exciting of sports. Anyway, I was looking down the course, planning my next shot or something, when [1]I saw these paragliders floating down from the heights. I thought to myself, that looks like fun. Perhaps I should have a go at it myself.

Interviewer: So you went on a course in France, I believe.

Hannah: That's right. I'd actually tried to go on a paragliding course in England a few years ago. I'd even paid the course fee – about £500 – but every time I went down to do the course, [2]it was either too windy or it was raining, so in the end I got fed up and asked for my money back. Anyway, looking on the Internet, I found this rather wonderful place, called Dune du Pyla on the coast in south-west France. It's actually the highest sand dune in Europe – and they run courses there. The price was a bit higher with the travel, but it was a really nice place, and [2]since sunshine was almost guaranteed, I went for it.

Interviewer: Great! And can you tell me, are there any advantages to jumping off a sand dune? I imagine it's rather less dangerous than jumping off a mountain, isn't it?

Hannah: Well, it isn't so high – only about 150 metres, in fact – but wherever you fall, it's going to hurt, so from that point of view, it doesn't necessarily make a lot of difference. [3]But the good thing is that the beach guarantees you a relatively soft landing. Too soft if you go off the beach and into the water, because then you'll need rescuing, although there's usually a steady breeze to keep you from going into the sea.

Interviewer: And what's the main difficulty for a beginner? I imagine it's taking off and landing.

Hannah: The major problem for a complete beginner like myself is actually [4]learning how to hold your paraglider up in the air – er, you know, so that both sides open properly. They only allow you to run off the edge and fly when you've mastered that technique, so I didn't get to fly till after lunch on my first day. Getting your paraglider open is quite tricky to start with. It makes you feel a bit silly when you see other people happily flying around below you or above you all morning!

Interviewer: And when you actually start flying, how does your teacher tell you what to do? Does he fly along beside you?

Hannah: No, it sounds a nice idea, and I'd have felt a lot safer if I'd had someone beside me. In fact, [5]I listened to my instructor, Chantalle, through an earphone – she stayed down below and spoke into a small microphone device to tell me what to do. It was generally very quiet, calm and civilised, except when she raised her voice to shout at other flyers to keep away from me. And then you really heard her!

Interviewer: And is landing a problem?

Hannah: Surprisingly not. I was expecting something rather violent – you know, I've come off a horse in my time and that's a lot rougher, I can tell you. This was a relatively soft landing – the sand cushions you a bit – so [6]hardly more of a bump than hopping off a park bench. And you're wearing a helmet, of course, rather like a biker's, so the danger's minimal.

Interviewer: But is it really as safe as you make out?

Hannah: They say it is. I mean, there are a couple of serious accidents every year, but the people I know who do it are very safety-conscious. Most sports, including slow earthbound ones like golf, have some element of risk – I've known a few people get hit by golf balls – some of my own even! [7]Most of all, though, I was taken by the silence. I mean, you're not disturbing anybody in your rather strange eccentric quest for thrills and new sensations. [7]That for me's the best thing and something I've rarely come across before.

Interviewer: Hannah, thank you.

Hannah: A pleasure.

Vocabulary

look, see, watch, listen and hear

1 **As a warmer** With books closed, write on the board:

- *look, see, watch*
- *listen, hear.*

Ask students to say how the words in each set are different. If students speak the same first language, ask them how each of the words is translated. Then ask them to do the exercise.

Answers
1 watching **2** looking; saw **3** listened **4** heard

2 If these words present a problem for your students, tell them to copy them into their notebooks and, when they are speaking or writing, to pay special attention to make sure they are using the words correctly.

Answers
1 looked at **2** watching **3** hear **4** looking at **5** see **6** watching **7** hear **8** listening to

Extension idea Ask students to write their own sentences to illustrate the differences between *look, see* and *watch* and *listen* and *hear.*

Speaking | Part 3

1 ***As a warmer*** Ask students if they remember what happens in Speaking Part 3. (They work in pairs and have to discuss options connected with an issue, then decide which option(s) would be best.)

When students look back to pages 37–38 in Unit 3, ask them particularly to look at the phrases they studied in Exercise 3, the strategies they considered in Exercise 6 and the phrases they studied in Exercise 7.

Tell students that when they do the task, they should try to use some of the phrases.

Give them some time to look at the task and think about what they want to say. In the live exam, they would have 15 seconds. Tell them they can talk about what would interest them personally, but they should also talk about what would interest different types of student, and why.

Give them two minutes to do this first part of the task.

2 ***Alternative treatment*** Before students follow the instructions in the book, ask them: *Which of these things should you do, and which should you avoid doing?* (Answers: **1** You can do this. However, in the context of all the points on this checklist, the note below is relevant*; **2** Do this; **3** Do this; **4** Do this if your partner is talking too much and not giving you a chance to participate, otherwise avoid doing it, as your partner may find it distracting; **5** Avoid this.)

* You can point out that no marks will be lost for not discussing all prompts, and it is probably better to do fewer prompts in more depth than to run round everything superficially. Candidates who make a genuine conversation of it – listen, respond, agree and disagree in a friendly way – will earn more marks than those who plan their next turn without listening to their partner, or those who take it in turns to deal with prompts rather than addressing one prompt together (i.e. they should not treat it as a series of long turns).

3

Answers
Miguel and Irene did 2, 3 and 4.

CD 1 Track 26

Examiner: I'd like you to imagine that your college is interested in getting students to do more sport. Here are some ideas they are thinking about and a question for you to discuss. First, you have some time to look at the task. Now talk to each other about why these ideas might encourage students to do more sport.

Irene: So, shall I start? How do you think a visit to the national athletics championship would encourage students to do more sport?

Miguel: Um well, perhaps seeing elite athletes doing their sports will inspire students to take up the sport and imitate them.

Irene: Yes, and I imagine students would see how fantastic these people look and how much they enjoy the activity.

Miguel: Maybe, but it might only interest some of the students, but not others. And what about a talk by a professional footballer? I suppose that might be interesting because he'll probably describe what life's really like for a footballer and how – what's the word – how glamorous he is.

Irene: I suppose so, but I don't think it would encourage me to start playing football myself. There are lots of people like me who aren't really interested in football at all.

Miguel: Yes, I see what you mean. And what about the next one – a weekend doing adventure sports? That's just the sort of thing I'd enjoy, and I think lots of students would get interested in adventure sports if they tried them.

Irene: That's a good point, and it could be a good, fun weekend, but do you really think many people are going to get involved in adventure sports as a result? They're quite expensive, you know, and you can't do them every day, not living in a big city.

Miguel: That's true – but you can always go to one of those sports centres with a … a climbing wall, I think it's called.

Irene: Maybe, but I don't think it's the same as going to the mountains to do these things, and not everyone can afford to do that. Now what about a school sports day? To me, that just sounds – mm, what's the word – childish. We used to do sports days at primary school.

Miguel: Well, perhaps this could be organised in a more adult way – you know, with some serious sports for people who were interested and less serious activities for other people. That way everyone could get involved.

Irene: Yes, good idea, and people could be organised into teams and it could all be made quite competitive and enjoyable at the same time. When I think about it, it could be really successful.

Miguel: You're right. And the idea of free membership of a sports club is also a great idea. Hm. Lots of students would be interested in that.

Irene: Yes, but I think that would mainly interest people who already do sports, so I'm not sure it would encourage other people to start.

Miguel: No … unless it was also a social club at the same time. I think that would be extremely effective.

Examiner: Thank you.

4 **Answers**
suggesting ideas: Well, perhaps …; I imagine students would see …; What about …?; I suppose that might be …
asking your partner's opinion: How do you think …?; Do you really think …?
agreeing: Yes, and …; Yes, I see what you mean; That's a good point, and …; That's true; Yes, good idea; You're right
disagreeing: Maybe, but …; I suppose so, but …; Yes, but …

Extension idea Ask students to do Exercise 1 again, trying to use some of the phrases they have just studied.

5 **Pronunciation:** intonation (2)

As a warmer Ask one student: *What did you do last weekend?* When the student has answered, you say *Really?* first with a flat intonation, then with an interested rise-fall intonation. Ask students: *Which way of saying 'really' sounds interested?*

Ask them to imitate your 'interested' way of saying *really,* either individually or as a class chorus.

1 ▶

Answers
See recording script.

CD 1 Track 27

Miguel: Well, perhaps this could be organised in a more adult way, you know, with some serious sports for people who were interested and less serious activities for other people. That way everyone could get involved.

Irene: Yes, good idea and people could be organised into teams and it could all be made quite competitive and enjoyable at the same time. When I think about it, it could be really successful.

2 Point out that English speakers tend to use intonation to express interest in a way which many other languages do not. Some students may feel somewhat inhibited about imitating English intonation. Depending on your teaching situation, you may prefer not to insist that students imitate the intonation exactly, but they should at least be aware of this feature of the language and ready to try it if they feel motivated to do so.

6 ***Alternative treatment*** Before students do this exercise, elicit good strategies for approaching the task. You can refer students back to page 37 in Unit 3 for ideas.

7 Give students some time to look back over this Speaking section and the Speaking section in Unit 3 before they start and to think about what they want to say.

When they have finished both parts, round up decisions with the whole class.

Extension idea Ask students to look at the checklist in Exercise 2 again and discuss how well they did the task. Round up comments with the whole class and discuss as necessary.

Writing | Part 2 An article

As a warmer With books closed, ask students: *Have you ever written an article for a magazine, newspaper or website? What was it about? Who were the readers? Have you ever written an article in English?*

1 When students have finished underlining, ask them: *What do you think the editors are looking for in an article?* (Possible answers: It will be interesting and informative for readers.)

> **Suggested underlining**
> college magazine, keep fit, sporting activity, form of exercise you enjoy, how you started, why, recommend it to other people, article

2 While students are discussing, ask them to note down the ideas they would like to use.

3

> **Answer**
> running past opponents, scoring points, playing in a team, it's a ball game, running and keeping fit

4 Point out (referring to paragraph 2) that if something is complicated, it might be better just to say it is complicated rather than get into a muddle trying to explain things.

> **Answers**
> **1** para. 2 **2** para. 1 **3** para. 3

Extension idea Ask students to write a brief plan for Nacho's article. (Suggested answer: Para. 1: How I started: at school; boys in winter, compulsory; athletic, more agile than others; Para. 2: description – complicated rules, any level – but need coach to be good; Para. 3: recommend if like ball games, running – good for spectators.)

5 ***Alternative treatment*** Go through the Language reference section with students before they do the exercise. Ask them to look at the examples in Nacho's article and link them to the explanation in the reference.

> **Answers**
> **1** Although **2** Despite **3** Although **4** despite
> **5** However **6** although **7** Despite **8** However

6 Remind students that they will achieve higher marks by using a range of appropriate vocabulary.

> **Answers**
> **1** competitive **2** rough **3** athletic **4** opponents
> **5** coach **6** spectators **7** trophy

7 ***Alternative treatment 1*** Ask students to write their plans in class. Give them about three minutes to do this. Tell them they can use ideas they had in Exercise 2 and a similar structure to Nacho's article.

When they have finished, ask them to compare their plans with a partner.

Alternative treatment 2 Tell students their articles will be published in the class magazine.

If you wish, you can ask them to write their articles on a computer and print them out.

Give them a deadline for handing in their articles, which you can either collate as a magazine or pin on the class noticeboard.

> **Answer**
> See sample answer in Exercise 3.

Extension idea If you did Alternative treatment 2, as a follow-up, ask students in small groups to discuss which are the two best articles and why. This will help other students to focus on what they can do to improve their own writing.

8 Dream of the stars

Unit objectives

- **Reading and Use of English Part 7:** practice in identifying key ideas in questions
- **Reading and Use of English Part 1:** reading the article quickly before answering the questions; advice on how to approach each question; paying attention to grammar as well as meaning
- **Writing Part 1:** writing an essay dealing with advantages and disadvantages; writing a balanced essay; writing the first sentence of a paragraph; linking words and phrases
- **Listening Part 2:** practice in predicting type of word and type of information
- **Speaking Part 4:** speaking in general; giving a balanced answer; expressing agreement and disagreement
- **Pronunciation:** grouping words and pausing (2)
- **Grammar:** *at, in* and *on* in phrases expressing location; reported speech
- **Vocabulary:** verb collocations with *ambition, career, experience* and *job*; confusion between *play, performance* and *acting*; *audience, (the) public* and *spectators*; *scene* and *stage*; words and phrases connected with arts and education, e.g. *a voluntary activity, work in a team,* etc.

Starting off

As a warmer Ask students in small groups: *What's happening in each of the photos? How important do you think it is in each of the professions in the photos for people to become famous and successful?*

If you wish, before they do the exercises in the book, ask them to quickly revise Making comparisons in the Language reference section on page 169.

1 and 2 *Extension idea* When students have finished, ask them to change groups and take turns to summarise the ideas they discussed.

Reading and Use of English | Part 7

1 ***Extension idea*** Say to students in groups: *Talk about your favourite actors and films and explain why you like them so much.*

2 ***Alternative treatment***

- Ask students to read the article but not the questions (they can cover the questions).
- They then work in pairs and must write one question for each actor on a piece of paper. The correct answer to each question must be only one actor.
- They then pass the questions to another pair to answer.
- When they have finished, ask students to look at the questions in the book and compare them with their questions. Which were similar and which were different?

Suggested underlining
1 accept negative comments **2** learned a lot from people already working **3** other people's suggestions improve their acting **4** excited, people watching **5** planned to enter a different profession **6** prefers, theatre **7** *Underline the whole question.* **8** worried about performing in front of some important people **9** tried to train, somewhere else **10** *Underline the whole question.*

3 **Answers**
1 E **2** D **3** E **4** B **5** C **6** C **7** A **8** A **9** D **10** B

4 As a follow-up question, you could ask students if they prefer performing in front of people they know or people they do not know.

Vocabulary

Verb collocations with *ambition, career, experience* and *job*

1 Ask students to check their answers by scanning back through the text.

Answers
1 pursue **2** achieve **3** offered **4** turn it down **5** gain

2 EP Tell students to copy these collocations into their notebooks.

Answers
1 experience **2** a job **3** a career **4** an ambition

3 Students should cover Exercise 2 while doing this exercise, then uncover it to check their answers.

Answers
1 make/pursue **2** achieve/fulfil/realise
3 gain/get **4** find / apply for / look for **5** build
6 offers **7** launches

4 ***Alternative treatment*** Students can talk about the ambitions and career of someone in their family if they prefer.

play, performance and *acting; audience, (the) public* and *spectators; scene* and *stage*

5 

Answers
1 plays **2** performance **3** acting **4** stage
5 an audience

6 Tell students they should pay special attention to these words in order to avoid making mistakes when speaking or writing.

Answers
2 play **3** acting **4** performance **5** audience
6 scene **7** stage **8** spectators

Extension idea Ask students to work in pairs and write five sentences using five of these words. When they write the sentence, they should leave a gap where the word should be. They then pass the sentences to another pair, who should write the correct word in each gap.

This would be a suitable moment to do the photocopiable activity for this unit on the Teacher's Resources CD-ROM.

Grammar

at, in and *on* in phrases expressing location

1 ***As a warmer*** With books closed, ask students what they remember of the reading text by asking these questions:

- *Where does the writer live?* (Answer: in Venice)
- *And where can he find fresh water?* (Answer: at a well in the centre of the square)
- *Where is his room?* (Answer: on the third floor)
- *Where does his sister live?* (Answer: in Spain)
- *Where does his uncle want to sell the book?* (Answer: in the market)

After they have done the exercise, go through the Language reference on page 172 with them.

Answers
1 in **2** in **3** on **4** at **5** at

2 Tell students that candidates make many mistakes with prepositions. When they have finished the exercise, ask them to check their answers in pairs using the Language reference section.

Answers
1 in **2** on **3** at **4** in **5** at; at; at **6** on **7** in; on
8 at **9** on **10** in; in

Listening | Part 2

As a warmer Ask students:

- *What different quiz shows are there on TV (in your country)?*
- *Which is your favourite?*
- *Which would you like to take part in?*

1 You can elicit possible answers for the first three questions, e.g.

- *Who do you think the producer invited?* – get suggestions (a relative, member of the family, friend, etc.)
- *What sort of feeling might someone have if they didn't want to go?* (embarrassed, nervous, uncomfortable, self-conscious, etc.)
- *What could this be? A means of transport? A piece of clothing?*, etc.

Alternative treatment Ask students to do this exercise alone and give them 45 seconds, as they would have in the live exam. After 45 seconds, they can either compare their ideas in pairs or you can round up with the whole class.

Suggested answers
1 a place, noun **2** a feeling, adjective **3** means of transport, noun **4** something he didn't bring, noun **5** something you learn, noun
6 a place, noun **7** noun describing an occupation **8** adjective, subject matter, noun **9** period of time, noun or adverb
10 a prize, noun

2 Before you play the recording, remind students they will need between one and three words for each gap.

Answers
1 shop **2** nervous **3** hired car **4** tie
5 trivial facts **6** Green Room **7** university lecturer **8** general knowledge **9** two months
10 (big) television/TV

Extension idea Photocopy the recording script from the Teacher's Resources CD-ROM. Write these phrases on the board:

it was the chance of a lifetime   by chance   there must have been quite a chance   get stuck in traffic   stood around

Play the recording again and ask students to underline or highlight the phrases as they listen.

They should then work in pairs and discuss what each phrase means in the context.

Finally, they check their answers by looking in a dictionary.

CD 1 Track 28

Julie: So, I'm going to tell you about my dad's ten minutes of fame. It was when he starred on a TV show a few years ago and it happened like this. The family had a small [1]shop just round the corner from where we live, and one day my aunt was working there on her own when a TV producer just happened to walk in and ask her if she'd like to take part in this quiz show called *The Big Question*. That was a big show, you remember, when we were small kids. I suppose he thought she'd look good on TV, sort of photogenic. Anyway, when she was asked, she just refused to even consider it. She said she was afraid she'd get so [2]nervous that she'd be unable to say a word when a question came to her! My elder sister, who was only 11 at the time, told her she should go because it was the chance of a lifetime, but no one could say anything that'd make her change her mind. Just by chance, at that moment, my dad walked in. Well, he saw his opportunity and offered to go on the show himself! Anyway, the producer agreed, and a couple of weeks later, my father took a [3]hired car – because ours was very old – and he drove to the TV studios. I don't think he trusted the trains to arrive on time, but I reckon there must have been quite a chance he'd get stuck in traffic. You know what it's like round London. Well, anyway, when he got there, he suddenly realised that he'd left his [4]tie behind, so he had to ask the producer if they'd got a spare one at the studio he could borrow. Anyway, he was told he didn't need one – or a jacket for that matter either. Oh, and I forgot to say, he didn't really study for the show – you know, by reading encyclopedias and so on. In fact, I don't think we've ever had an encyclopedia in the house, though I did suggest buying one for the occasion. I suppose he could've gone online, but as far as I know, he didn't. He told me later that, the only thing he'd done was what he always did in the evening, which was read the popular press that we hadn't sold during the day and pick up lots of [5]trivial facts.

Anyway, later, what he told me was that before the show, he stood around with the other participants in somewhere called 'The [6]Green Room', where they chatted to each other and were given something to eat and drink, and they got to know each other a bit. My dad felt a bit intimidated, I think, because the other competitors seemed very confident and looked really keen. My dad was expecting them to be doctors or lawyers or something, but in fact, although one of the women really was a [7]university lecturer, the others were a bus driver and somebody who worked in a bank, so quite a mixture. When the show started, I think my dad felt quite lucky and very surprised to be able to answer his questions, which were all about [8]general knowledge and nothing too specialist, because he actually managed to win. Anyway, he did the show, which was recorded, and all of us were longing to see him in it, especially as we knew he'd won. We thought it'd be broadcast like the following week, so it'd be really up to date, but in fact it came on nearly [9]two months later and we almost missed it because we'd almost forgotten about it by then. But it was good, because for weeks, after people were stopping my dad in the street and saying, 'Didn't I see you on *The Big Question*?' Finally though, my dad didn't become a millionaire or come home in a sports car unfortunately, but he did win a [10]big television with a wide screen – we've still got it at home, and it's great for the football – and a big fluffy elephant, which he gave to me. They were pretty impressive prizes for us then – well, for me, because I was still quite small. So, that was my dad's ten minutes of fame. I wonder what mine'll be.

3 Ask also: *Julie said it was 'the chance of a lifetime'. Do you agree? Why? / Why not?*

Extension idea Ask students in groups to discuss:

- *If you won a holiday at a place you could choose, where would you go?*
- *If you won a house in a place you could choose, where would you choose to have your house?*

Grammar

Reported speech

As a warmer Ask students to work in small groups and think of times when they have used reported speech in their own language. Ask them to think about why they used reported speech rather than reporting things using direct speech. (Suggested answer: Reported speech summarises the main points of a conversation and is therefore more efficient and less time-consuming; it allows speakers to report the meaning when they cannot remember the exact words.)

1 Ask students to work in pairs and briefly report in English a conversation they had in their own language recently.

Answers
1 a **2** b

2 If necessary, go through the Language reference section on page 173 (Reported speech) before students do this exercise.

Answers
1 previous night he had seen **2** she would (get/come) back **3** would arrive (on/in) **4** wasn't allowed to borrow **5** (had) made several mistakes **6** (had) found the play

Extension idea Ask students to work in pairs and write five sentences in direct speech on a piece of paper. Tell them not to write questions. They then pass the paper to another pair of students who put them into reported speech.

3 Tell students that we often use reporting verbs other than *say* or *tell* to report what was said more exactly. Point out that many of these verbs can be followed by either the infinitive or a verb + *-ing*.

After students have done the exercise, they can check their answers either by looking at the recording script if they have access to it, or by consulting the Language reference section.

Answers
1 to even consider **2** to go **3** if they'd got **4** buying

4 **Answers**
1 stealing / that she had stolen **2** lying **3** to buy **4** breaking **5** to visit **6** to buy **7** to visit **8** installing **9** to send **10** not to use

Extension idea Ask students, perhaps for homework, to write their own example sentences for each of the reporting verbs in this exercise.

5 **Answers**
1 advised him to see **2** suggested going swimming that **3** told me to switch off **4** reminded Natasha to post **5** of not taking any **6** to do her best

Reading and Use of English | Part 1

1 ***As a warmer*** With books closed, ask students in small groups:

- *How is the Internet changing the way we get our entertainment?*
- *What entertainment do you get from the Internet?*

Students can talk about downloading films and music, watching things on YouTube, internet gaming and using social media to interact with friends.

Extension idea Ask students to share their favourite YouTube videos and to recommend videos to each other.

2 Remind students that they should quickly skim the text before they look at the questions.

Answers
Through advertisements

3 **Answers**
1 B **2** C **3** A **4** C **5** A **6** D **7** D **8** B

4 Tell students that obviously in the live exam there will be no clues, but that here they are intended to help them look at the sort of things which will give them the answers: meaning, collocation, fixed phrases, etc.

5 Students should take turns to describe what they have uploaded or would like to upload.

Speaking | Part 4

As a warmer With books closed, ask students in small groups: *What arts subjects, dance, music, painting and so on, have you studied at school? How useful have these subjects been for you?*

1 ▶ With books open, draw students' attention to the exercise rubric and tell them that in fact they will often be asked general questions of opinion rather than personal questions.

Play the recording as they read.

Answers
generally speaking, generally, on the whole

Extension idea Ask students to highlight phrases Antonia and Peter use to introduce their opinions. (Answers: *I think*, *I guess*, *I feel*)

CD 1 Track 29

Examiner: Do you think schools should teach subjects such as dance, drama or music?

Antonia: Well, / I think generally speaking / schools should teach these subjects to small children / so that they can find out / if they like them. / I think these subjects / help children to learn / how to express themselves. / But I don't think generally it's so important for older children / or teenagers to do these subjects because / they tend to have lots of other things to study. / So, / on the whole, / I guess these subjects should be / voluntary, / not compulsory, / as children get older.

Examiner: Peter, do you agree with Antonia?

Peter: Generally, yes, but / I feel it's a pity when students / don't have time / for the subjects they enjoy.

2 Remind students that it is not essential to give a balanced answer to these questions, although it will impress the examiners if they can. It is essential to support your opinions with reasons and/or examples.

Answers and suggested answers
1 She talks about teaching young children these subjects and then balances it with *but* and her views on older children and teenagers.
2 Young children: to discover if they like the subjects and to learn self-expression; Older children and teenagers: so many other subjects to study.
3 b

Extension idea: Ask students in pairs to say if they agree with Antonia and Peter.

3 Give students some time to study the language Antonia and Peter use in Exercise 1 and think how to frame their answers.

4 Pronunciation: grouping words and pausing (2)

1 and 2 Remind students that there are no fixed rules for when to pause, though it is natural to pause between words which form a group of meaning, i.e. native speakers pause to choose the words which will go together to express their ideas; they do not generally pause to choose grammar words, which come more naturally to them.

Answers
See the recording script for Track 29.

3 and 4 Encourage students not to exaggerate the pauses, so that they sound as fluent as possible.

5 EP If you have not already done so, photocopy the word list for students to refer to as they do this exercise.

Tell them they may be able to use some phrases with more than one question.

Suggested answers
1 a compulsory/voluntary activity, develop musical abilities, develop artistic expression, develop their musical knowledge
2 develop their artistic expression, work in a team
3 interrupt a film with advertisements, when the film is released
4 a celebrity, avoid/cause a scandal, disturb/protect someone's privacy, the media, a tabloid (newspaper)
5 help society develop, make people aware of problems

6 Tell students they need not use the phrases from Exercise 5 unless they wish to.

Give them some time to think about and prepare their answers.

Alternative treatment Ask students to look at the questions in Exercise 2 while they are listening to their partners answering the questions. When they have finished answering all the questions, tell them to use the questions to give their partner some feedback on how well they did.

Extension idea Round up with the whole class by asking the same questions randomly to students around the class and then eliciting or suggesting ways in which they might be able to improve their answers.

Writing | Part 1 An essay

As a warmer With books closed, ask students:

- *Why do you think people are so interested in hearing about the lives of celebrities and other well-known people?*
- *Would you like to be famous? Why? / Why not?*

1 With books still closed, tell students that they are going to look at a writing task in this lesson. Ask: *What is the first thing you should do when you read a writing task?* (Answer: Underline key ideas) *Why?* (Answer: To make sure you know what you are being asked and that you cover all parts of the question.)

Students then do the exercise in the book.

> **Suggested underlining**
> famous, film star, both advantages and disadvantages, media attention, lifestyle, your own idea

2 To help the discussion, ask students to think about how being famous might:

- help an actor's career
- affect their private life.

3 ***Extension idea*** When students have finished, ask them to exchange their plans with a partner. Tell students they should look at the plans and consider these things (you can write them on the board):

- *Does the plan cover all parts of the task in Exercise 1?*
- *Do you think it covers the most important aspects of the topic?*
- *Does the outline look logical?*

When students are ready, they can discuss the plans with their partners and make any changes to their own plan that they wish.

4 Ask students to think about the teachers' comments on opening paragraphs in Unit 5, then make comments to their partners about their paragraphs.

5 Point out that this opening paragraph has the advantage that it is brief, allowing the student more space to discuss the subject in the main body of the essay.

6 As you go through the answers to the questions with students, point out that when they write, they always need to be thinking of their reader(s). They should ask themselves:

- *Have I expressed my ideas clearly?*
- *Is it easy for the reader to navigate their way through the essay?*
- *When they've finished reading, is it clear what my opinion is?*

Tell them that if the answer to all these questions is 'yes', then they are probably achieving their aims.

Suggested answers

2

	advantages (para. 1)	disadvantages (para. 2)
1	if actors are well-known … they will be offered more jobs	film stars have little privacy or time to themselves
2	they live exciting and glamorous lives with plenty of foreign travel and luxury	people with glamorous lifestyles meet other glamorous people and this can sometimes cause problems with, for example, their family relationships
3	fame and success go together	they have to work very hard to be successful and this may lead to considerable stress

3 The underlined sentences and phrase say what the paragraph will contain. This helps the reader know where the essay is going.

4 *Students should highlight:*
However, which, Firstly, if, and if, Also, with, Finally, On the other hand, First, because, Next, and this, Finally, and this, To conclude, because, However

5 in the final paragraph

6 It is required by the writing task, which asks *Do you agree?*

7 Tell students when they do this to use Javier's essay in Exercise 6 as a model.

8 ***Alternative treatment*** After students have underlined, ask them to discuss the advantages and disadvantages of a career in music or acting in groups, or as a whole class.

Ask them to note down key points in their discussion as they discuss.

They can then work in pairs or small groups to write a plan for their essays.

Finally, for homework, they can write their answers.

Sample answer
Many young people's ambition is to go into the music industry or the theatre. However, careers in these fields have both advantages and disadvantages.
There are two main advantages to these professions. Firstly, you can earn a living from a hobby. For example, if you enjoy playing a musical instrument, becoming a member of a band or an orchestra appears to be the perfect job. The second advantage is that if you are successful, you may become famous, and people will admire you for your professional abilities.
However, there are also two disadvantages. Being well known means that you may have less privacy. Many actors, for example, are continually followed by photographers, so they have to be very careful what they do or say in public. Also, the majority of actors and musicians do not earn very much money from their work and may have to teach music or drama in order to survive.
In my opinion, unless you are very talented, the best thing is to pursue your music or acting interests as free-time activities and concentrate on studying for a safer, more conventional profession instead.

Vocabulary and grammar review Unit 7

1 **1** unpredictable **2** patience **3** preparations **4** inexperienced **5** simply **6** unwilling **7** realistic **8** valuable

2 **1** taking **2** to get **3** to invite **4** changing **5** to have **6** stealing **7** to finish **8** to become **9** working **10** asking **11** working **12** spending

3 **1** aren't allowed / are not allowed to go **2** to avoid getting **3** can't bear windsurfing **4** you mind turning **5** you (may) risk having **6** no/little point (in) going

Vocabulary and grammar review Unit 8

1 **1** C **2** B **3** A **4** C **5** A **6** D **7** C **8** B

2 **1** Although / Even though **2** despite / in spite of **3** While/Whereas **4** Despite / In spite of **5** However **6** while/whereas **7** although / even though **8** while/whereas

3 **1** of the danger **2** the tickets were expensive **3** despite not feeling (very) **4** even though her salary is **5** she had slept the / she had been asleep the **6** would call at/after the

Secrets of the mind

Unit objectives

- **Reading and Use of English Part 5:** skimming; finding and understanding the relevant section of text before looking at the alternatives; explaining references and phrases from context
- **Reading and Use of English Part 4:** identifying what grammar, vocabulary, etc. is required; revision of language from previous units
- **Writing Part 2:** writing a report; making recommendations and suggestions
- **Listening Part 1:** linking key words on the recording with correct alternatives; listening for gist and global meaning
- **Speaking Part 2:** speculating and comparing
- **Pronunciation:** sentence stress (3)
- **Grammar:** modal verbs to express certainty and possibility
- **Vocabulary:** confusion between *achieve, carry out* and *devote; stay, spend* and *pass; make, cause* and *have*; collocations with *cause; look, seem* and *appear; a bit, slightly, rather*

Starting off

1 ***As a warmer*** With books closed, ask students in small groups to brainstorm things which make them happy or would make them happy.

They then do the exercise.

Answers
1 c **2** a **3** b **4** g **5** d **6** e **7** h **8** f **9** i

Extension idea Ask students: *Which of the things in this exercise did you mention before you opened your books (as a warmer)?*

2 ***Alternative treatment*** Ask students: *Which are the three most essential and the three least important?*

Suggestions for other things which may make people happy: good health, personal freedom, a generally happy social environment, a happy disposition, etc.

Extension idea Ask students to work in pairs and talk about the happiest time of their lives. When was it? Why were they so happy?

3 This exercise is similar to Speaking Part 2.

Give each student a minute to speak.

You can follow up with a question for the student who is listening: *Which situation would you find most enjoyable?*

Reading and Use of English | Part 5

1 Give students two minutes to do this – be strict about the timing to encourage skimming. Tell them before they start that they should not try to understand every word, but to read quickly to get the general ideas which will answer the question.

Alternative treatment Tell students to look for three things or three factors which make people happy.

Answers
The writer thinks happiness comes from: earning enough money to live comfortably; having a challenging job and/or pursuing an absorbing hobby; from concentrating hard on something

2 Remind students how in Unit 6 in Reading and Use of English Part 5 (page 65) they read the question, then found the answer in the text and then looked at the four alternatives A–D. This activity also encourages them to follow this procedure; tell them to make sure they understand the underlined section before reading the alternatives.

Answers
1 C **2** C

3 Encourage students to follow the same technique as in Exercise 2, i.e. finding and understanding the relevant section of the text before looking at the alternatives, then underlining the words in the text which gave them the answer.

Answers
3 D **4** A **5** B **6** A

4 ***Alternative treatment*** Ask students: *Are the things mentioned in the text things which would make you happy? Why? / Why not?*

Vocabulary

achieve, carry out and *devote*

1 **Answers**
1 achieve 2 devoted 3 carrying out

2 **Answers**
1 achieve: an aim, an ambition, an objective, success
2 carry out: an improvement, an instruction, an order, research, a test, a threat
3 devote: energy, one's life, time

3 **Answers**
1 achieved; ambition 2 carrying out research/ tests 3 devote; time 4 devoted; energy
5 carry out; threat 6 carry out orders/instructions

stay, spend and *pass; make, cause* and *have*

4 Ask students to look at the dictionary definitions and elicit why *have* is the correct answer to question 1. (Answer: have an effect / have an impact) Point out that question 1 really deals with a collocation, though this may not be the case with the other questions, which they should do in pairs.

Answers
1 have 2 caused 3 spent 4 spent 5 stay 6 made

5 Tell students to check when they use these words in their writing and speaking, so as to avoid mistakes.

Answers
1 spend 2 pass 3 stay 4 had/made 5 spend
6 spent 7 causing 8 makes/made 9 have
10 spent

Extension idea Ask students to write their own example for each of the six words.

6 **Answers**
make: a change, an impact, an impression, trouble
cause: an accident, a problem, trouble
have: an effect, an impact, an impression, a problem

7 **Answers**
1 caused an accident 2 made; impression
3 caused; (any) trouble / problems / a problem
4 have the impression 5 makes / made / has made; change 5 have; impact/effect

Listening | Part 1

1 To get students started, ask them to look at the first statement and elicit what other things we could base first opinions (or impressions) on, e.g. looks, facial expressions, clothes, body language, etc. Ask students to discuss how important each of them is. For all discussion points, ask students to give examples and talk from personal experience.

2 You can point out to students that predicting possible vocabulary before they listen will improve their performance in this type of task.

Suggested answers
1A intonation **1B** body language, appearance, gestures, mirror **1C** actual words
2A character **2B** people we like **2C** things in common, hobbies

3 

Answers
1 B 2 C
Words and phrases used: appearance, intonation, mirror, things in common, character

CD 2 Track 02

Presenter: One. You hear an expert giving advice about meeting people for the first time.

Dr Bazey: When you meet people for the first time, there's a general belief that it's the words you use that count most, so people tend to spend lots of time preparing how they're going to start a conversation – you know, their opening gambit, so to speak. However, [1]research shows that before we've even opened our mouths, people've already made up their minds about us just from our appearance alone. Then after that, it's things like our intonation and the tone of our voice. Our choice of words actually counts for very little. So, time spent in front of the mirror is probably time well spent!

Presenter: Two. You hear a man and a woman talking about a successful relationship.

Mandy: So, Rob, congratulations! Still happily together after 25 years! What's the secret?

Rob: No secret, really. A bit of give and take and consideration for each other. I mean, even if we don't get on with all of each other's friends, at least we put up with them and don't show it. We don't take each other for granted, and [2]we have lots of things in common – I'd say that's vital – things we enjoy doing together. Not that we're too alike in terms of character. I mean, I'm rather outgoing and dominating and I tend to go to extremes, while Liz is the more sensitive, cautious type. But that probably helps because I think we complement each other quite well.

4 Remind students to:

- underline the key idea in the question before they listen
- listen to the whole of each extract before they choose an answer. Sometimes the answer will depend on gist or global meaning.

Answers
3 B **4** C **5** C **6** A **7** B **8** B

CD 2 Track 03

Presenter: Three. You hear a psychologist in the UK talking about intelligence.

Psychologist: Psychology's quite a young science, which means psychologists haven't had time to measure how or whether our minds are evolving, or whether in fact we're getting cleverer. It's hard to prove that our intelligence is actually increasing, even if [3]young people nowadays tend to get higher marks in intelligence tests than they did 50 or 60 years ago. There are a variety of factors which could have an impact on this: better diets, our minds are stimulated more, or just getting more practice in tests of this type. At the same time, many people think that while exam results have been improving across the country, that's because the exams themselves aren't as demanding as they used to be.

Presenter: Four. You overhear a boy calling a friend on his mobile phone.

Jess: Hi, Ade.

Ade: Oh, hi there, Jess.

Jess: Um, Ade. I was (*yawns*) ... Sorry, I'm just so tired.

Ade: Oh, me too – who wouldn't be after all those mid-year tests we've been doing!

Jess: Yeah, I've been up studying most nights, so sorry if I haven't been all that friendly.

Ade: No problem. Anyway, you weren't irritable with me, so I don't mind. [4]Look, can we meet up some day next week instead of tomorrow, 'cos my mum's just told me I've got a dentist's appointment?

Jess: Poor you. Have you got a toothache or something?

Ade: No, just my annual check-up.

Jess: Oh, that's all right, then. Let's catch up at school, shall we?

Ade OK, see you then. Bye.

Presenter: Five. You overhear a man talking about things which frighten people.

Man: Oh, yeah, you know, [5]I'll do anything to avoid them.

Woman: Including going up several flights of stairs?

Man: Oh, yes. I mean, I just won't go in them, so I sometimes arrive at places a bit breathless.

Woman: I bet!

Man: I think I must have got the problem when I got trapped in one as a kid. I can't have been there for more than ten minutes, but I was trembling when I came out. It's totally irrational, because we all know that they're completely safe. I suppose it's like planes – I mean they terrify lots of people, though statistically they're very safe.

Woman: Well, see you upstairs, then!

Presenter: Six. You hear a girl talking to a boy about a dream.

Boy: Have you ever had a recurring dream – you know, one of those dreams which repeats itself from time to time?

Girl: Yeah, I have, actually. I'm in one of those high places, a mountain top or the top of a building, and suddenly, for no reason, I'm falling. It's terrifying because I fall for some time, but then suddenly I wake up.

Boy: Wow, that's weird. Do you think it means anything?

Girl: Well, [6]the interpretation I've read is that it's some sort of fear of failure. You know, there are all sorts of interpretations for other dreams. For example, that you could find something subconsciously threatening and your dream might be sort of pointing that out to you.

Presenter: Seven. You overhear two students talking about a classmate.

Rob: Cathy's been behaving a bit strangely lately, hasn't she? I mean, she's been very quiet and not talking much.

Ellie: Yes, she looks pretty stressed out and I guess it's been giving her bad nights.

Rob: What's the problem, do you know? Is it to do with her exams or something?

Ellie: Well, she had a maths exam last week, so she must have studied hard for it. But she's always been pretty hard-working, so she can't have got stressed by that. Anyway, she finds maths easy.

Rob: Lucky her! Hey, do you think she might've had a row with her boyfriend? He can be a bit difficult sometimes, don't you think?

Ellie: Yeah, it must be something like that. Now you come to mention it, I haven't seen him around recently. [7]Perhaps we'd better ask her about him.

Rob: And try and cheer her up.

Presenter: Eight. You hear a boy and a girl talking about the boy's free-time activities.

Boy: I read this thing on the Internet that says your free-time activities say lots about you. If you like sport, you probably like being with other people. On the other hand, [8]I'm someone who prefers doing things on his own, like playing computer games, and that probably shows the opposite, you know, that I'd rather be by myself.

Girl: And you don't feel so comfortable with other people, you mean?

Boy: Hmm, could be. Then again, people who enjoy travelling are often people who like taking risks, doing new things, if you see what I mean.

Girl: Well, you're obviously a stay-at-home type.

Boy: I sure am.

5 ***Alternative treatment*** Ask students to choose one of the two questions and prepare a short one-minute talk on it. Give them a minute or two to think of ideas and make a few notes. They then take turns to give their talks in pairs or small groups.

This would be a suitable moment to do the photocopiable activity for this unit on the Teacher's Resources CD-ROM.

Grammar

Modal verbs to express certainty and possibility

1 You can ask students to look at the first extract and ask these questions:

- *Does 'must' here express an obligation – something it's necessary to do – or does it express something the speaker is certain about?* (Answer: Something he is certain about)
- *Does 'can't' express something the speaker isn't able to do, or something he's sure is not true?* (Answer: Something he's sure is not true)

Go through the notes in the Language reference section on page 170 (Modal verbs – Expressing certainty and possibility) with the students.

Answers
1 1 must **2** can't **3**, **4** and **5** may, might, could
2 Present: *may* and *could*; past: *must have* and *can't have*.

2 If your students all speak the same first language, discuss the typical mistakes they make with modal verbs, e.g. following them all with infinitive + *to*.

Answers
1 ~~may have~~ must have **2** ~~mustn't be tired~~ can't be tired **3** ~~can have~~ may/might/could have
4 correct **5** ~~can't~~ must

3 Point out that modals expressing certainty and possibility about the past are all followed by *have* + past participle.

Answers
1 must have worked **2** must be **3** must have had / must have been having **4** may/might/could have had to; may/might/could have stopped
5 can't be **6** may/might/could rain

4 ***Alternative treatment*** You can say clearly absurd things about the pictures to provoke students to correct you, e.g. about the first picture: *She must be a professional dancer; She must have made a political speech.*

Suggested answer
In the first picture, the girl must have just performed at a concert because she's bowing to the audience and holding a violin. She must have played well, because the audience looks really enthusiastic. It might be a school concert and the audience may be parents and teachers. She must be feeling very pleased and she could also be feeling quite relieved that her performance went well.
In the second picture, the two boys must have broken the window while they were playing football. The man looks as if he might be going to tell them off or punish them. The boys may be feeling embarrassed about what they've done, or they could even be a bit frightened of the man's reaction. The man may be a little bit angry, but he might also remember his childhood and think that this was just an accident.

Reading and Use of English | Part 4

1 The grammar and vocabulary in this exercise come from areas covered in Units 8 and 9. Tell students that the questions test different aspects of grammar and vocabulary: they must identify what is being tested.

To remind them of things to avoid when doing this task, you can ask them these questions:

- *How many words can you write in the space?* (Answer: Between two and five)
- *Is it necessary to use the word given?* (Answer: Yes)
- *Can you change the word given, e.g. make it past or make it plural?* (Answer: No)

Answers
1 **a** This is more than five words.
b correct
c It's correct English, and it means the same, but it doesn't use *had*.
2 **a** *despite* is not followed by *of*
b correct
c *despite* is followed by a noun or a verb + *-ing*, not a verb in a tense
3 **a** doesn't use the word given
b *remind* means 'make someone aware of something they (may) have forgotten'.
c correct
4 **a** The answer contains six words – the maximum is five.
b The word given should not be changed in any way.
c correct
5 **a** *collected up* is not correct in this context.
b *taken up* is not the correct phrasal verb and does not use the word given.
c correct – *picked up* means 'collected'.
6 **a** *do* is not used with *effort*.
b correct
c *advise* is followed by an infinitive.

2 **Answers**
1 stand people making a noise **2** reminded him to lock **3** didn't / did not manage to see **4** can't/cannot have been **5** did you spend writing **6** may have found

Speaking | Part 2

As a warmer With books closed, ask students to discuss in pairs:

- *What things do you have to do which you find difficult?*
- *How do you feel when you're doing those difficult things?*
- *Why?*

1 With books open, point out to students that sometimes they cannot be completely certain what is happening in a photo, so they may have to speculate, which is what Peter is doing.

Alternative treatment Ask students in pairs to take turns to do the speaking task, i.e. compare the photos and say how they think the people are feeling about these difficult activities, before they do the exercise in the book.

2 After doing the exercise, go through the Language reference section on page 170 with students.

Answers
1 seem **2** must **3** perhaps **4** very different **5** exactly what **6** could be **7** who appears **8** may have decided **9** looks as if **10** unlike

Extension idea If you didn't do the Alternative treatment in Exercise 1, you can ask students to do the speaking task from Exercise 1 themselves now, covering over Peter's answer in Exercise 1 and practising using some of the language they have just studied.

CD 2 Track 04
See page 102 of the Student's Book.

3 Encourage students to suggest different possibilities for each sentence.

Suggested answers
1 they are celebrating the old man's birthday party. **2** very happy. **3** sing 'Happy Birthday' to him. **4** at a football match. **5** cheering their team. **6** they're outside and making a lot of noise. **7** really happy.

Extension idea When they have finished, ask students to change partners and compare their ideas with another student.

4 **Pronunciation:** sentence stress (3)

As a warmer: Read the sentence below twice but with the different emphasis indicated by the underlining:

Maria did her driving test yesterday. (underlined: driving test)

Maria did her driving test yesterday. (underlined: yesterday)

Ask: *What is the difference in emphasis between the two sentences? How does it change the message?* (Answer: In the first, the emphasis on *driving test* suggests she did not do something else we might have understood her to have done; in the second, the emphasis on *yesterday* points out that she did not do the test at another time.)

1

Answers
See recording script for Track 05 for words to underline.
In a), he emphasises the fact that he's speculating, while in b), he emphasises the different possible activities.

CD 2 Track 05

a The girl seems to be working with equipment in a factory. I'm not sure exactly what she's doing, but she could be building a machine or something.

b The girl seems to be working with equipment in a factory. I'm not sure exactly what she's doing, but she could be building a machine or something.

2 Students can also give feedback on how accurately their partner emphasises the underlined words.

3 

Answers
See recording script for Track 06 for words to underline. The boy (A) sounds more certain about what he is saying. The girl (B) sounds less certain and emphasises that she is speculating.

CD 2 Track 06

A: The girl in the first photo may have decided to climb the mountain because she wants a new experience, or perhaps she just enjoys being in the mountains even though she looks a bit tired. The girl in the second photo looks as if she's starting a new job and learning to do something. She looks as if she's quite warm from her work, unlike the girl in the first photo.

B: The girl in the first photo may have decided to climb the mountain because she wants a new experience, or perhaps she just enjoys being in the mountains even though she looks a bit tired. The girl in the second photo looks as if she's starting a new job and learning to do something. She looks as if she's quite warm from her work, unlike the girl in the first photo.

4 ***Extension idea*** Ask students: *Did you emphasise the same words? How was the meaning of what you both read different?*

5 Point out to students that stress is a very useful tool for emphasis and communication, and that using it well will make their speaking much more effective.

Ask the student who is listening to give feedback on how natural and/or effective their partner sounds when using emphatic stress.

5 Tell students that speakers do tend to use words/phrases like *a little, a bit, slightly*, etc. to modify adjectives, and that by using them, their speaking will sound more natural.

Answers
a bit, quite

6 ***Alternative treatment*** Ask students while they listen to their partners to note down the words they emphasise as they are speaking.

When they have finished, tell them to tell each other which words they particularly emphasised.

7 Between tasks, round up feedback from the whole class and discuss it, so that students have a chance to apply it in the second task.

Writing | Part 2 A report

1 ***As a warmer*** Ask students:

- *Does your/this school have a student committee or student representatives on a school council?*
- *What sort of things do they discuss?*
- *What sort of things do the students ask for or recommend to the school directors? Why?*
- *How effective do you think the student representatives are?*

Alternative treatment Tell students they are going to work on writing a report. Before they start, ask them:

- *How might the format of a report be different from other types of writing you do?* (Answer: It will have a title, may be divided into sections with section headings.)
- *What is the purpose of a report?* (Answer: To inform about things which have happened, or the present situation and, possibly, to make recommendations/suggestions.)

Ask students to look at the Writing section in Unit 3 on page 39 to remind them about what they have already learned about report writing.

Suggested underlining
improving the classrooms, students' social activities, director of your college, report describing the benefits of both ideas, which one you think should be chosen and why

2 **Answers**
1 the director of your college **2** formal
3 benefits of both ideas, which should be chosen and why

3 **Answers**
1 discuss **2** spent **3** make **4** contains **5** find
6 benefit **7** improve **8** participate **9** reduce
10 recommend

Extension idea Tell students that many of the verbs in the box are quite formal. Write these less formal verbs on the board and ask students to match them with more formal ones in the box:

be better have cut make better take part talk about

(Answers: be better – benefit; have – contain; cut – reduce; make better – improve; take part – participate; talk about – discuss)

4 **Suggested answers**

1 The writer recommends new furniture and an air-conditioning system.
2 He/She can look at the section headings and find what he/she needs.
3 Yes
4 The *Introduction* states the purpose of the report, *The classrooms* talks about the need for improvements, *Social activities* about the effect of the money on these, *Recommendation* makes a recommendation for spending the money and gives a reason.
5 The present tense to talk about the present situation and the conditional to talk about the effects if the money were spent in the ways suggested.
6 No – it uses a formal style, as appropriate in a report.

Extension idea Ask students to read the report again and underline words and phrases they think would be useful when they write a report. Tell them to copy these into their notebooks.

5 **Answers**
1 installing **2** spending **3** buy **4** to equip

6 ***Alternative treatment*** Divide the class into two groups. Tell them there is also a large sum of money available for their college (you can suggest an amount if you wish) and that they are members of the student committee.

Tell students to work in pairs and make a list of things they would like the money to be spent on.

They then put their ideas to the committee and discuss which four recommendations they should make to the directors of the college.

Finally, each student writes their four recommendations and compares their sentences with their partners.

7 When students have finished discussing, round up ideas with the whole class and discuss any issues which arise.

Alternative treatment If you did not do the alternative treatment for Exercise 6, you could do it now – it might be too much to do it twice.

8 If you wish to replicate exam conditions, tell students that they should do this exercise in 40 minutes, which is what they will have in the live exam.

Alternative treatment Especially with weaker classes, ask students to do the preparatory steps, i.e. underlining and writing a plan in pairs in class and discuss their plans with them before they do the actual writing.

Suggested underlining
large amount of money available to spend on improving the neighbourhood where you live, town council, making recommendations

Sample answer

Improvements to the Palmar District

Introduction
The aim of this report is to suggest how the town can spend the money which it has available for improving this district.

The streets
The Palmar District is an old part of the city with narrow streets and pavements. Because the pavements are so narrow, it is difficult for pedestrians to walk together or pass each other without stepping into the road, which can be dangerous. Also, many of the streets are badly lit at night, which means that it can be quite frightening to walk there.

The traffic
Unfortunately, the district has a lot of traffic, which makes it very noisy and polluted. Also there is very little space available for residents to park their cars.

Recommendations
It would be a good idea to make some of the main streets for pedestrians only, with wider pavements. I also suggest that the council should provide good street lights and build a car park for residents. Finally, I recommend that the town council should build a ring road so that traffic does not have to enter the neighbourhood.

Spend, spend, spend?

Unit objectives

- **Reading and Use of English Part 2:** skimming the text; identifying the type of word needed
- **Reading and Use of English Part 5:** skimming; practising exam technique
- **Writing Part 2:** writing a review; using linking words and discourse markers; writing longer, more complex sentences
- **Listening Part 4:** listening for gist and detail
- **Speaking Part 1:** strategies for dealing with Part 1 questions
- **Pronunciation:** linking (1)
- **Grammar:** *as* and *like*; modal verbs expressing ability
- **Vocabulary:** *arrive, get* and *reach*; phrasal verbs, e.g. *come up with, pull in,* etc.; words connected with shopping: *a bargain, a brand,* etc.

Starting off

1 ***As a warmer*** Before students open their books, ask them to brainstorm a list of different types of shop and then choose their three favourites.

2 ***Extension idea 1*** Ask students to discuss in small groups: *How much money should parents give their children as a weekly allowance, when the children are:*

- *12 years old?*
- *16 years old?*
- *18 years old?*

Extension idea 2 Divide the class into an even number of pairs or small groups to prepare and do a role play. Tell them:

- *half the pairs or groups will play the role of children*
- *the other half will play the role of their parents.*

Tell them:

- *the children want to buy something expensive but quite useful, e.g. a new tablet computer, a new bicycle, a trip to London to practise their English, or something else*
- *the children should work together in pairs or small groups to prepare their roles: they should decide what they want to buy, how much it will cost and how they are going to try to persuade their 'parents' to pay for it*
- *the parents should work together in pairs or small groups to prepare their roles: their children are always asking for more money to buy things. They should think of reasons why they do not want to give their children more money and ways in which the children can get the money they need.*

Ask children and parents to discuss the situation together, either in pairs or in groups of four to sort out the situation.

Finally, round up by asking each pair/group to report the result of their discussion to the whole class.

Reading and Use of English | Part 2

1 ***Alternative treatment*** Two of the questions in this section test *as* and *like*. If you wish, do the Grammar section on *as* and *like* before you do this section.

As a warmer With books closed, ask students in small groups to discuss: *How are shopping habits and trends changing? What trends have you noticed over the last few years?* (Suggested answers: At the time of writing, there are continuing trends towards more out-of-town shopping in large shopping centres, closure of traditional high-street shops, more specialist, quality, boutique-style shops and a large increase in online shopping. Also, people often use shops to look at products which they later buy online.)

2 When students finish, ask them to work in pairs and summarise their answers.

Answers
Local shops: personal service, social relationships, more satisfying experience
Shopping online: discount prices, 24/7 shopping and deliveries

3 Remind students to decide what type of word they need for each gap. Also, they should read the completed text to check it makes sense.

If you did the alternative treatment suggested in Exercise 1, if necessary for question 6 ask: *Does the article say shops should be clubs, or similar to clubs?*

For question 7, would shops be seen to be unique, or similar to something which is unique?

For question 8, point out that *experience* is uncountable when talking in general about things you learn from (e.g. qualifications and experience), but when talking about a particular event which affects you, it is countable.

Answers
1 which **2** up **3** but **4** According **5** much
6 like **7** as **8** a

Extension idea Ask students: *What is the writer's solution to the problems of local shops? Do you agree with it?* (Answer: The writer suggests personal service, a social relationship, each shop being different, opening when customers are not working, giving customers a better experience than they would have online.)

4 You can also ask students: *Do you sometimes look at products in shops, then buy them online?*

Grammar

as and *like*

1 *As* and *like* are often confused: in many languages, they are translated by the same word. When students have answered the question, go through the notes in the Language reference section on page 163 (*as* and *like*) with them.

Answers
1 as **2** like

2 Ask students to highlight *the same as* in question 3 and *such as* in question 9 when they have finished the exercise.

Answers
1 as **2** as **3** as **4** like **5** as **6** as; as **7** as
8 like **9** as; as **10** as

Extension idea After students have done the exercise, ask them to work in pairs and write five other similar sentences but leaving a gap for *as* or *like*. They then read their sentences to another pair, who have to say whether *as* or *like* should go in the gaps.

Reading and Use of English | Part 5

1 ***As a warmer*** Ask students to look at the picture.

Ask them in pairs to describe what is happening.

Ask them to look at the title of the reading text (*My greatest influence*). Ask them in pairs: *What do you think might be the connection between the picture and the text (without reading)?*

Students will have to speculate about the possible connection and come up with ideas and suggestions. When they have finished, round up their ideas with the whole class and possibly ask them to vote which is the most likely.

Alternative treatment If you did the warmer, omit the questions in this exercise in the book and go straight to Exercise 2.

2 Tell students that this text comes from a magazine written by and for teenagers in the United States.

Give students two minutes to do the exercise and be strict about the timing. When they have finished, ask them to work in pairs and:

- summarise the story
- say what the writer's greatest influence is/was.

3 Before they start, elicit that the best method of dealing with multiple-choice questions is to:

- underline the key idea in the question
- find, read and understand the section of the text which provides the answer
- read the options and choose the one which matches what the text says.

Answers
1 B **2** D **3** B **4** C **5** C **6** A

Extension idea Ask students in small groups: *If one of your teachers asked you to write an essay with the title 'My greatest influence', who or what would you write about, and why?*

4 **Answers**
1 b **2** b **3** a **4** a **5** b **6** a **7** a **8** a **9** b

5 ***Alternative treatment*** Ask students to react to the text. Here are some of the questions you could ask (you can write these on the board):

- *What impression do you have of Rachel?*
- *Do you think she has a difficult life? Why? / Why not?*
- *Do you think the lesson she learned from the homeless man was a valuable one?*
- *Do you think you learn more from people whose situation is worse than yours or better than yours?*

Vocabulary

arrive, *get* and *reach*

1 Tell students that candidates frequently confuse these words, so they should take special care when using them.

Answers
1 get **2** arrived **3** reached

2 **Answers**
1 reached **2** get **3** gets/arrives **4** get
5 arrived **6** reach

Extension idea With books closed, ask students to write three sentences of their own using these words.

3 **Answers**
1 safe and sound **2** in time **3** on time **4** shortly
5 unannounced **6** finally

Listening | Part 4

1 ***As a warmer*** Tell students in groups to look at the photos and ask them to describe what they see. Ask them: *Is it similar to or different from shopping areas in your town? In what ways?*

To get students started, you can elicit some of the advantages and disadvantages listed below from the whole class.

Suggested answers
There are many shops in one place, easy parking, places to relax, customers are protected from the weather, etc., there is usually good security, so customers feel safe.

2 Tell students to take notes while they listen.

Answers
Reasons the interviewees mention: access (station and motorway), good shops, good quality, caters for every taste including people who don't want to shop, family fun, safe and crime free, luxurious surroundings, reduce family conflicts.

CD 2 Track 07

Interviewer: Hi! I'm in a new shopping centre with some guys who've been finding out a bit more about the place. Kerry?

Kerry: Yeah – first, let me tell you where it is. You know you'd expect to drive for miles out into the countryside to a place among green fields. When they build them in the country, everyone has to get there by car, but at least then the parking's easy. [1] This new one's taken over some abandoned industrial land on the outskirts of the city and it's pulling in young people, families, everyone, so there's a really great atmosphere.

Interviewer: So why do you think they went for this particular site? Salim?

Salim: Well, apparently, they were offered a place in the country and the plans were approved, but [2]they chose this place for its convenient access from the station and the motorway. The locals did start kicking up a fuss about traffic noise and fumes and that sort of thing, so it took quite a long time to get things started, but they managed to get permission in the end.

Interviewer: But why do you think there are such masses of people here now? What's behind its popularity?

Salim: Well, you see, people don't just come to shop. They come to spend the day. There are tons of good stores with branches here, so even though you end up spending quite a bit, in general the stuff's good quality and [3]there's something here for everyone. It caters for every taste, including people like myself who'd rather not shop at all but would prefer to take in a film or hit the gym instead. [3]So you see lots of families having fun here too, without having to hang around with each other the whole time. Dad goes off to look at sports equipment or electronics, while mum hunts for clothes. You know, that sort of thing.

Interviewer: From where I'm standing now I can see trees and fountains. There are cafés, music for chilling out and even a free fashion show. It's a bit of a change from your normal high street, isn't it?

Kerry: Yeah, it's incredible, isn't it? You know, these places are pretty safe – I mean, I know some rough lads come here, but with all the security staff around, there's never any trouble. [4]But what I really like is that the place feels a bit like a palace. You know, I can spend all day here with my friends surrounded by all this expensive stuff without it costing me a penny. People treat you pretty well and you don't have to spend anything unless you want to.

Interviewer: We're always hearing about families having arguments when they go shopping. Why's that?

Salim: Apparently, [5]it's because they're spending the day together and their tastes in how to spend their free time are different, so they get irritable with each other, and this breaks down into arguments about which shops to go to and so on.

Interviewer: And this place is organised to cater for different tastes, isn't it?

Kerry: Well, yeah, [6]what they've done is organise the shops, cafés and other places so there's a wide range of quite different shops in each section. This means that families can still be fairly close to each other, even though they're up to different things. You know, mum can wander into the clothes shop if that's what she wants to do, while dad can pop into the computer shop next door and the kids can go to a games shop or a music shop. They're all nearby and they can find each other easily.

Interviewer: And what else have they done, Salim?

Salim: Well, they've come up with ways of making shopping less tiring. You know, a day's shopping wears people out. They thought of hiring out small electrically driven cars to shoppers to cut down the amount they walk. They came up against problems of space – there just wasn't enough room for them all – so they also thought about those moving walkways you see at airports and that would've involved redesigning everything. [7]What they actually came up with is a new technology which sends everything you've bought to your exit point, and you just pick it up there.

Interviewer: Awesome. Thanks, Kerry and Salim.

Kerry: Cheers.

3 Ask students to work in pairs and discuss what they think are the answers to each question.

Alternative treatment for Exercises 2 and 3 Skip Exercise 2 and ask students to treat Exercise 3 as an exam task.

Give them one minute to read and underline the questions before you play the recording twice.

4 Play the recording again for students to check and complete their answers.

Answers (Exercises 3 and 4)
1 B **2** C **3** B **4** A **5** A **6** B **7** C

Extension idea Print out and photocopy the recording script from the Teacher's Resources CD-ROM. Play the recording again and ask students to check their answers as they listen and read.

5 ***Extension idea*** Ask students to work alone and make a short shopping list of different things they would like to buy (maximum five items). Then ask them to work in small groups and plan a shopping trip together in their own town or this town. Tell them they should decide:

- how much time they need
- which shops to visit
- when and where to meet.

Vocabulary

Phrasal verbs

1 Point out that some of the phrasal verbs are quite colloquial (*hang around, chill out, pop into*) so are unlikely to be tested in Reading and Use of English, though students might well hear them in the Listening paper and certainly from native speakers.

Alternative treatment If you have not already done so, print and photocopy the recording script for Listening Part 4 (Track 07).

Ask students to find each of the phrasal verbs in the script and, in pairs, to discuss what each of them means in the context.

They then do the matching exercise to check their answers.

Answers
1 j **2** a **3** g **4** h **5** l **6** k **7** d **8** f **9** c **10** e **11** i **12** b

2 ***Extension idea*** When students have completed the sentences, ask them to work in pairs and write five more sentences with gaps where the phrasal verbs should be. They then pass their sentences to another pair to answer.

Answers
1 came up with **2** cut down on **3** pop into **4** caters for **5** hanging around with **6** wore us out **7** pulling in **8** taken over **9** come up against **10** pick up **11** been up to **12** chill out

Grammar

Modals expressing ability

1 The main confusion is with *could* and *was/were able to* in the affirmative. You may wish to highlight that:

- *could* expresses a general ability in the past; it does not say whether the thing was actually done or happened on a particular occasion
- *was/were able to* expresses the idea that someone actually did the thing on a particular occasion.

Alternatively, you can sort this out by going through the Language reference section on page 170 with them.

Answers
1 d; f **2** c; g **3** a; e **4** b; h

2 When students have finished the exercise, ask them to write four of their own sentences using *can, could, was able to* and *could have*.

Answers
1 were able to **2** couldn't sleep **3** could **4** Can you **5** could have bought **6** were able to

3 Tell students that, if necessary, they should refer to the Vocabulary section on page 111 as they answer. Ask them to compare their answers in pairs before rounding up with the whole class.

Answers
1 able to cut down **2** you could have had **3** you able to pick up **4** cannot/can't cater for such

4 ***Alternative treatment*** Elicit the mistake in sentence 1 and its correction. (Answer: *can't* is wrong and should be replaced by *couldn't* or *wasn't able to*.) Tell students that candidates frequently use *can* when talking about the past; this is a mistake due to carelessness which they should avoid.

When going through the exercise with students, elicit why each sentence is wrong.

Answers
1 ~~can't~~ couldn't / wasn't able to **2** ~~could~~ was able to OR ~~that I could~~ to be able to **3** ~~can~~ could **4** ~~could~~ can **5** ~~can~~ could **6** ~~could~~ were able to **7** correct **8** ~~could~~ can

This would be a suitable moment to do the photocopiable activity on the Teacher's Resources CD-ROM.

Speaking | Part 1

1 ***As a warmer*** With books closed, elicit from students what happens in Speaking Part 1. (Answer: Candidates answer questions about themselves, the things they do and like, their family and neighbourhood, etc.)

Tell students: *The theme of this unit is money and shopping. Work in pairs and think of three Part 1 questions you think you might be asked in the exam connected with money and shopping.*

Give students a few minutes to write their questions. They then change partners and take turns to ask and answer their questions.

With books open, give students a little time to think of answers to the questions in the exercise.

2 Ask students: *Why are all of these good strategies for answering Part 1 questions?* (Answer: Because they all involve giving quite long answers and show students' ability to structure an informative answer.)

Alternative treatment Print out and photocopy the recording script for this exercise from the Teacher's Resources CD-ROM. Students can then follow it as they do the exercise.

Answers
1 P **2** B **3** P **4** I

CD 2 Track 08

Examiner: Peter, what things do you enjoy spending money on?

Peter: Well, like many young people in my country, I'm a big football fan. I support Bayern Munich and I try to go to all their home matches and a few away matches when I don't have too much school work. So that's what I really like spending money on: my season ticket to Bayern.

Examiner: And Irene, what do teenagers in your country typically spend their money on?

Irene: I think it really depends, because girls_and boys typically spend their money a bit differently. I guess girls spend more money on clothes_and magazines, while boys spend more money_on music_and things like football matches. In general though, I think both boys_and girls spend_a lot_of money just going_out to places_and having_a good time.

Examiner: Peter, do you have a favourite shop?

Peter: Hmm, I'd have to think, because I'm not too keen on shopping, actually. Um, there is one shop I really enjoy going to. It's one of a chain of sports shops and what I really like about it is just to wander round and see all the clothes and equipment they sell. I see things for sports I don't do but I'd like to try, and that gives me the idea that one day I could try the sport, when I can afford the clothes and equipment, I mean.

Examiner: Irene. Is there anything you'd like to buy that you can't afford?

Irene: Of course! Lots of things! I mean, I don't have a lot of money. My parents give me an allowance, and other people in my family give me money for my birthday and at other times. At the moment, I'm saving up for a better computer – I'd like to study IT when I go to university.

3 ***Alternative treatment*** If you have photocopied the recording script, ask students to underline or note down words and phrases they would like to use before they start as part of their planning.

4 Pronunciation: linking (1)

1 Play the example sentence several times and give students a chance to practise saying it themselves. Similarly, play Irene's speech several times.

CD 2 Track 09

He understood, but didn't answer.

I like eating and talking.

I don't often buy clothes and shoes.

2 

CD 2 Track 10

Irene: I think it really depends, because girls and boys typically spend their money a bit differently. I guess girls spend more money on clothes and magazines, while boys spend more money on music and things like football matches. In general though, I think both boys and girls spend a lot of money just going out to places and having a good time.

3 Students can take turns to read individual sentences from Irene's answer.

Answers
1 We don't pronounce final 't's and 'd's when the word which follows begins with a consonant.
2 We link the word to the following word when the word ends with a consonant and the following word begins with a vowel.

4 **Answers**
See recording script for Track 10.

5 Tell students their answers should be several lines long, like Irene's and Peter's.

Answers
See recording script for Track 11.

CD 2 Track 11

Peter: Hmm, I'd have to think because I'm not too keen on shopping actually. Um, there is one shop I really enjoy going to. It's one of a chain of sports shops and what I really like about it is just to wander round and see all the clothes and equipment they sell. I see things for sports I don't do but I'd like to try, and that gives me the idea that one day I could try the sport, when I can afford the clothes and equipment, I mean.

6 Give students two or three minutes to write their answers and plan their pronunciation.

5 **Answers**
1 Peter uses strategy 1; Irene uses strategy 3.

CD 2 Track 12

Examiner: Peter, what's shopping like in the area where you live?

Peter: I'm not sure, because I don't do a lot of shopping, at least not where I live. There's a place where they sell snacks and takeaways that I quite like – I've been there a few times with my mates – and I guess the shopping must be pretty good, because my mum and dad do all the shopping locally and they never complain!

Examiner: And Irene, what's shopping like in the area where you live?

Irene: I think it's really good. My dad and I love cooking together at weekends and doing these really exotic dishes, and there are plenty of shops in the area which sell good vegetables, food from different parts of the world, and spices and things, so we can find all our ingredients locally. My dad's a great cook. I'm learning a lot from him and we have a great time together!

6 ***Alternative treatment*** Print out and photocopy the word list from the Teacher's Resources CD-ROM. Students can then check the meanings of the words while they link them to questions.

Extension idea Ask students in pairs to think of ten more useful words/phrases connected with shopping which they could use when answering the questions.

When they have finished, ask them to compare their words/phrases with another pair of students.

Finally, round up with the whole class and write the vocabulary on the board. Students can copy useful words/phrases in their notebooks.

7 Encourage students to use the strategies outlined in Exercise 2 and vocabulary from Exercise 6.

Alternative treatment Tell students they must use each of the strategies at least once when answering the questions.

When they are listening to their partner speaking, they should decide which strategy is being used and how successfully their partner is answering the question.

Afterwards, they should give each other feedback.

You should then round up feedback on this and also feedback on how easy it is to answer these questions, and discuss / sort out any difficulties.

Writing | Part 2 A review

As a warmer Ask students in small groups to look at the photos. Ask: *Which of these places do you have in or near your town? / Which of these places exist in or near this town? Which of them are good places for people your age to go to have a good time? What sort of things can people do there?*

1 **Suggested underlining**
website for visitors, visitors to our town, enjoy, place in or near our town / people your age, meeting up, having a good time, review, type of place, what do there, how to find, why recommend

2 Tell students to take notes as they speak.

3 Tell students to make sure they have covered all the points they have underlined in the task in Exercise 1.

4 **Suggested answers**
Para. 1: Place – Cinecity – activities available
Para. 2: Most popular activities – mention karaoke
Para. 3: Location + using the underground
Para. 4: Why I recommend it

Extension idea Ask students to compare the plan they wrote for Eva's review with their own. Tell them they can make any changes they want to their own plan.

5 Tell students they should try to imitate the structures in Eva's review while they do the exercise.

Alternative treatment Before they do the exercise, ask students in pairs: *Which of these words and phrases can be used for joining sentences to form longer or more complex sentences?* (Answers: where, to, apart from, although, because, even if, but don't worry if, because, is probably the best way to)

Ask students to look at the two remaining phrases, *in fact* and *what is more*. Ask: *Which phrase introduces something which the reader may find surprising?* (Answer: in fact) *What does 'what is more' mean?* (Answer: also)

Suggested answers
2 Apart from three roller coasters, there is a tunnel of horrors, a terror swing and many other rides.
3 Although the theme park is quite expensive, it's well worth the entrance fee, which includes all the attractions.
4 If you bring your swimsuit, one of the best attractions is a waterslide, where you slide more than 100 metres into a bubbling pool.
5 Funtime is about 10 kilometres from the town centre, but if you don't have a car don't worry because you can get there by bus.
6 In fact, taking the bus is probably the best way to avoid parking problems.
7 I would recommend Funtime because there is such a huge variety of attractions that everyone who goes there will be entertained.
8 What is more, you can get a weekend pass, which is an entrance ticket for the whole weekend, so you will have time to visit every attraction.

Extension idea Ask students to write sentences of their own about places in their town using the same words and phrases.

6 Remind students to write following their plans.

Sample answer
See sample answer in Student's Book Exercise 4.

Vocabulary and grammar review Unit 9

1 **1** spent **2** have **3** causes **4** pass **5** had **6** made **7** spent

2 **1** may be **2** could just **3** might be doing it **4** very different **5** look **6** appear to **7** look as if **8** perhaps **9** both

3 **1** must have switched **2** can't have turned **3** may not have heard **4** could have left **5** might answer **6** might have forgotten **7** can't have forgotten

Vocabulary and grammar review Unit 10

1 **1** C **2** B **3** D **4** A **5** C **6** B **7** B **8** A

2 **1** was not / wasn't able to finish **2** down (on) the amount of **3** was/felt so worn out by **4** could not / couldn't come up with **5** able to pick Paz up **6** get to the cinema until

3 **1** as **2** as **3** as **4** as **5** like **6** as **7** as **8** Like **9** like **10** like

Medical matters

Unit objectives

- **Reading and Use of English Part 6:** understanding text structure; identifying and interpreting reference
- **Reading and Use of English Part 3:** adding negative prefixes
- **Writing Part 1:** writing an essay; brainstorming; writing concluding paragraphs, including examples; using relative clauses
- **Listening Part 3:** listening for global meaning, gist and detail
- **Speaking Part 2:** strategies and phrases for getting out of difficulties and finding the right word
- **Pronunciation:** intonation (3)
- **Grammar:** relative pronouns and relative clauses
- **Vocabulary:** words connected with health: *illness, treatment, infection, prescription, diagnose,* etc.; guessing the meanings of idiomatic expressions from context: *rub shoulders with, feel off-colour,* etc.

Starting off

1 ***As a warmer*** With books closed, follow these steps:

- Ask students to work in groups and decide on a definition of what it means to be healthy. Ask them to write their ideas down.
- They then compare their different definitions with the rest of the class.
- They open their books and read the statements in the book (1–6) to see which is closest to their definition.

When students have done the exercise in the book, do not check the answers together, as this will be done in Exercise 3.

2 ▶ Pause the recording between speakers to give students time to discuss and match up the extracts. If necessary, play the recording twice.

CD 2 Tracks 13 and 14

Speaker A: I really do believe in a healthy mind in a healthy body, so I get up pretty early, about 6.30. / I do an hour's workout in the morning before going to college, and in the evening, I usually have time for a couple of hours' sport, so I really think I'm very fit.

Speaker B: I take my health pretty seriously. I think you have to. / I visit the doctor regularly once a year for a check-up. Once or twice I've needed treatment for something she's found, but it's never been anything very serious.

Speaker C: I think I'm healthy, but then I take good care of myself because I believe that old saying: 'Everything in moderation'. So / I'm very careful to eat a balanced diet – only a little meat and plenty of fresh fruit and vegetables – and I'm careful about not putting on weight, so I do a reasonable amount of exercise as well.

Speaker D: I think I'm pretty healthy. I mean, I have a lovely life. I've been retired now for nearly 20 years on a nice pension, so no financial problems, and / here I am, in my 80s, still quite active – I mean, I go shopping, visit my friends and go to the cinema when I want to. What more can you ask for?

Speaker E: I'm just a naturally happy, relaxed person and I think that's a large part of the secret of good health. / I never go to the doctor and in fact, I don't even know my doctor's name. I'm lucky: I've never had a day's illness in my life.

Speaker F: Me, healthy? I should think so. I've never been stopped from doing anything I want to do because of an illness. Of course, / I do catch the occasional cold or other infection. I'm a doctor, so I can't really avoid them, but I get over them pretty quickly and they don't usually stop me going to work

3 ▶ See recording script for Tracks 13 and 14.

Answers (Exercises 1 and 2)

1 **1** active **2** workout **3** catch; infection; get over **4** check-up; treatment **5** illness **6** balanced diet; putting on

2 **A** 2 **B** 4 **C** 6 **D** 1 **E** 5 **F** 3

Extension idea Ask students to copy useful vocabulary into their notebooks.

If you wish, photocopy the word list for this unit from the Teacher's Resources CD-ROM for students to check meanings.

4 ***Extension idea*** Ask students to work in small groups and:

- brainstorm a list of things people can do to stay healthy
- decide which three are the most important
- change groups and compare ideas.

Listening | Part 3

1 ***As a warmer*** Tell students to look at the photo. Ask:

- *What is happening in the photo?* (Answer: A man is having his blood pressure checked by a doctor.)
- *How important is it for people to visit their doctor regularly?*

Answers
1 five; eight **2** read and think about the meaning of each option **3** express the same idea

2 **Answers**
1 g **2** d **3** f **4** h **5** c **6** b **7** i **8** e **9** a

3 ***Alternative treatment*** If you wish to give your students exam practice, omit this exercise.

Answers
Speaker 1: surgery, prescribe, treat
Speaker 2: cure(d), diagnose
Speaker 3: examination, vaccination, sick note
Speaker 4: examination
Speaker 5: heal

CD 2 Track 15

Speaker 1: Well, I got to the surgery at a quarter past eight for an appointment at eight-thirty, but in fact I had to hang around there till nearly half past nine to see him, so I was feeling pretty uptight, because there were only a couple of other people ahead of me. I mean, I only had a sore throat – so I was with the doctor for about a couple of minutes. Anyway, he said I'd just got a slight infection, which is what I was expecting, and he prescribed some antibiotics to treat it. But I did find it a bit annoying to have to wait so long, especially as I was missing my favourite class of the week!

Speaker 2: I've been feeling a bit off-colour for some time now and I've been to the doctor several times to try to get to the bottom of it. Anyway, this time my doctor was so sympathetic. She asked me all sorts of questions about my medical history and my family background and she took lots of notes. She spent a really long time and sounded so interested that when I left, I felt almost cured! Not that she was able to diagnose my problem straight away, but she did send me off for tests.

Speaker 3: My mum sent me to see the doctor the other day because I thought I'd got the flu and needed a few days off school. Anyway, the doctor gave me quite a thorough examination and then she told me I was hardly ill at all and that I should've had a vaccination and she refused to give me a sick note. Frankly, I was amazed and pretty annoyed, because I'd been coughing and sneezing all week and feeling very under the weather. Anyway, there was nothing I could do to change her mind, so it was back to school the same morning, worse luck!

Speaker 4: When I went in, my doctor just asked me a few questions but she didn't examine me. Then she prescribed me some pills and said that if the symptoms persisted, I should come back the following week. I told her I wanted a proper examination straight away and I stayed there sitting in my chair. I must say she looked a bit taken aback, but then she got up from her desk and came and gave me a really thorough check-up. In the end, she apologised and said she'd been up all night on duty in the local hospital.

Speaker 5: I went to my doctor complaining of neck pains and I was there for what seemed like hours. She gave me a very complete check-up and took ages over it. She looked at my neck, asked about my medical history and my daily routine. Then she told me that the problem was probably caused by too much sitting in front of the computer studying, and with a good rest, my neck would heal itself. She suggested that I should take time off to unwind and then the pain would just go away on its own.

4 Remind students that they should underline the key ideas as they read the questions.

Suggested underlining
A wasn't given enough attention **B** needed to relax **C** irritated **D** wish, hadn't gone **E** felt better after, visit **F** asked for a specialist **G** agreed, diagnosis **H** arrived late

Alternative treatment 1 Ask students how many questions they can already answer from doing Exercise 3.

Alternative treatment 2 Ask students to note down which speaker (1–5) uses each word/phrase from Exercise 2.

Answers
1 G **2** E **3** C **4** A **5** B

5 ***Alternative treatment*** Discuss these questions with the whole class.

Reading and Use of English | Part 6

1 ***As a warmer*** Ask students in small groups to look at the photos. Ask them: *The photos show aspects of life as a medical student. What aspects do the photos show?* (Answers: Visiting patients with a medical team, studying hard and probably memorising large amounts of information.)

2 Before they start reading, ask students: *Why is it a good idea to make notes in the margin while you read?* (Answers: To keep track of the developing structure of the text so that when students read the missing sentences, it will help them to know where to look to place them.)

Alternative treatment As it is getting towards the end of the course, good time management for the exam is becoming important. Give students five minutes to complete this exercise on their own and be strict about the time limit.

When the five minutes are up, ask students to compare their notes in pairs.

Suggested answers
Para. 2: tutorials
Para. 3: extra degree + academic research
Para. 4: being a clinical student
Para. 5: clinical training, part of a team
Para. 6: conclusion

3 **Suggested underlining (and reference)**
B opportunity to do many things (what things?) **C** the different specialties (what specialties?), the three years (which three years?) **D** the team (what team?) **E** I was expected to work extremely hard (by whom? where?) **F** These well-known people (who are they?) **G** *This* meant (who/what does *this* refer to?)

Alternative treatment (Exercises 3 and 4) Ask students to work alone and do this exercise and Exercise 4 at the same time, working methodically through the sentences one by one as they did in previous units and as they would do in the exam.

If you follow this treatment, give students a time limit of eight minutes and be strict about the limit.

Students can compare their answers in pairs when they finish.

4 **Answers**
1 G **2** A **3** F **4** C **5** B **6** D

5 ***Extension idea*** For students who do not want to study medicine, ask them to discuss in small groups: *What do you want to study at university? What do you think studying this subject involves? Try to describe some of the aspects of the experience and what you expect.*

Vocabulary

Idiomatic expressions

Alternative treatment Photocopy the recording script for Track 15 from the Teacher's Resources CD-ROM. Ask students to find the expressions in the reading text and the recording script so that they can work out the meanings with more context.

Answers
1 c **2** a **3** d **4** b **5** e **6** f **7** g

Extension idea Divide the class into two groups. Each group should think of six idiomatic expressions they already know. The groups then take it in turns to say one of their expressions and challenge the other groups to say what it means. If they do so correctly, they get a point. If they are worng or they do not know, the first group gets a point. You should act as referee. The group with the most points wins.

Grammar

Relative pronouns and relative clauses

1 In sentence 5, *which* would also be a correct answer. If you wish, elicit that *which* and *that* are interchangeable in defining relative clauses.

Answers
1 who **2** whose **3** which **4** where **5** that/which

2 Before doing this exercise, go through the notes in the Language reference section on page 172 (Relative pronouns and relative clauses) with students. When doing the exercise, do not let students just rely on whether there are commas or no commas to decide whether the clauses are defining or non-defining. Ask them: *Is the information in the relative clause essential to understand who or what we are talking about, or is it just extra information? Why?* For example, in sentence 1, unless we say *where I go for my holidays,* we do not know which village is being talked about. In sentence 2, we already know who we are talking about because her name is given, so *who you met on the train* is extra information.

Answers
1 D **2** ND **3** D **4** D **5** ND **6** D

3 Remind students of the rule that *that* can be used instead of *who* or *which* in defining relative clauses, but not in non-defining relative clauses.

Answers
3, 4 and 6

4 **Answers**
3 and 4, because they are the object of the clause.

Extension idea Ask students to write five sentences of their own as examples of different rules for relative clauses. They should refer to the Language reference section on page 172 (Relative pronouns and relative clauses) to do this.

5 Tell students that it is important to avoid these mistakes when writing or speaking and that they should pay attention when checking their written work. Tell them also that using relative clauses appropriately in the Writing paper will gain them marks, as it shows their range of grammar and their ability to write more complex sentences.

Answers
1 ~~it's~~ which **2** ~~his~~ whose **3** ~~that~~ which **4** ~~you wrote it last week~~ you wrote last week **5** ~~who you met them this morning~~ who you met this morning **6** ~~that~~ what **7** ~~which it has a view~~ which has a view **8** ~~which it won~~ which won

6 **Answers**

2 He studied hard for his maths exam, which he found quite easy. / He found the maths exam, which he studied hard for, quite easy.
3 The man (who/that) they sold the car to is a taxi driver. / They sold the car to a man who is a taxi driver.
4 Could you give me the newspaper (which/that) you were reading earlier?
5 That white house over there is the house where he was born.
6 Where's the envelope (which/that) I put the money in?
7 Every morning I go running in the park with Patricia, whose brother you know.
8 Karen and Teresa, whose dog we're looking after, are on holiday in the Caribbean at the moment.

This would be a suitable moment to print out and do the photocopiable activity for this unit on the Teacher's Resources CD-ROM.

Reading and Use of English | Part 3

1 ***As a warmer***

Write *misuse* on the board and ask students to work in pairs and brainstorm other words beginning with the prefix *mis-*.

If you want to make it a game, the winning pair is the one with the most correct words.

Write the correct words they suggest on the board.

Follow up by asking students to suggest the meaning of *mis-* (Answer: wrongly/badly).

Answers
1 a

2 **Answers**
1 b **2** a

3 **Answers**
mis-: it means *to do something wrongly*

4 Point out that these are isolated sentences, whereas in the exam there will be a paragraph with gaps to complete.

Draw students' attention to spelling, e.g. of *disappoint* – a common spelling mistake is **dissapoint** – and *misspell* – remind them that the base word is *spell* and by adding the prefix *mis-*, the word then has a double 's'.

Remind students that in this part of the exam, words must be spelled correctly.

Answers
1 undo **2** disappoint **3** misuse **4** untie **5** misspell **6** disappeared **7** undressed **8** misinformed

5 EP ***Extension idea*** Ask students to write five sentences, each using one of the words in its negative form. They should leave the gap for the word blank. They then pass their sentences to another student, who should write the correct word in the gap.

Answers
inability/disability, disagreement, disappear, unaware, uncertain, inexperienced, informal, unhappiness, unhelpful, dishonest, dislike/unlike, impatient, unpredictable, unreliable, dissatisfied/unsatisfied, misunderstand

6 EP Point out that students do not just need negative forms in this exercise.

When they have finished, ask them to check their answers and their spelling in pairs.

Answers
1 unexpected **2** security **3** occasionally
4 medical **5** height **6** calculation **7** assistance
8 uneasy

Speaking | Part 2

1 ***As a warmer*** With books closed, ask students in small groups: *What problems can you have when you do speaking tasks in the exam, for example you can't think of a word?*

Students then brainstorm possible problems – these may include not understanding the examiner's instructions, making a mistake, getting nervous and freezing, having a partner in the exam who talks too much or not enough, etc.

Round up the problems they suggest and discuss possible solutions to each.

With books open, students should do the exercise.

Point out to them that they will not lose marks in the exam for any of these situations if they deal with them appropriately. Dealing with them appropriately demonstrates their ability to manage difficulties in English.

Suggested answers
When you need time to think: Let me think …
When you can't think of the word: I can't think of the word, but it's a type of …; I'm not sure how to say it, but it's used for …; What's the word?
When you've made a mistake: I'm sorry, what I meant was …; No, I mean …; What I want to say is that …; Sorry, I mean …

2 ▶ Before students listen, ask them in pairs to look at the checklist and say why each of the seven points are good things to do in the exam.

Answers
Antonia did all the things on the checklist.

Extension idea Ask students to say which phrases from Exercise 1 Antonia used.

CD 2 Track 16

Examiner: In this part of the test, I'm going to give each of you two photographs. I'd like you to talk about your photographs on your own for about a minute, and also to answer a question about your partner's photographs. Antonia, it's your turn first. Here are your photographs. They show people doing healthy activities. I'd like you to compare the photographs and say how important you think each activity is for staying healthy. All right?

Antonia: OK, so both photographs show people doing things which might be good for their sanity, sorry, I mean their health. In the first photo, I can see someone who looks as if he's, what's the word, he's commuting by bicycle in busy traffic. So, he's getting some exercise, which must be good for his general fitness. In the second photo, there are some young people who are doing some cooking – well, not exactly cooking because what they're doing is preparing a salad. What I want to say is, they're going to eat something quite healthy. I mean, it's not like eating pizza or hamburgers. So both photos show people doing something healthy – getting exercise and eating a good deeat, sorry, I mean diet. I'd say there are some problems with the idea of health in the first photo because of the danger from the traffic, especially because he's cycling in the night, I mean in the dark, and the, I can't think of the word, but it's a type of smoke which comes from the cars. On the other hand, if you live in the city, it's a good way of getting exercise. In the second photo, the kids should remember that they need to eat a mixed, um, sorry, a balanced diet, not just salad and fruit.

Examiner: Thank you.

3 **Answers**
2 a Nikolai **b** Miguel **c** Peter

4 **Pronunciation:** intonation **(3)**

1 ▶ Ask students to read the introductory information before they do this exercise. Point out that they are being asked to identify which words Antonia stresses because this is where most of the intonation takes place, i.e. stress and intonation are closely related.

Answers
See recording script for Track 17.

CD 2 Track 17

Antonia: OK, so both photographs show people doing things which might be good for their sanity, sorry, I mean their health. In the first photo I can see someone who looks as if he's, what's the word, he's commuting by bicycle in busy traffic.

2 ▶ Students should not worry that their answers coincide with the introduction to the pronunciation – this is simply reinforcement.

Answers
The speaker is more confident in a). Her voice falls on the final stressed words. In b), her voice rises on the final stressed words, making her sound uncertain.

CD 2 Track 18

a OK, so both photographs show people doing things which might be good for their sanity, sorry, I mean their health. In the first photo I can see someone who looks as if he's, what's the word, he's commuting by bicycle in busy traffic.

b OK, so both photographs show people doing things which might be good for their sanity, sorry, I mean their health. In the first photo I can see someone who looks as if he's, what's the word, he's commuting by bicycle in busy traffic.

3 Tell students they should choose which intonation they wish to use. If their partner identifies their intonation correctly, this shows that they have used it successfully.

4 ▶

Answers
See recording script for Track 19.

CD 2 Track 19

a I'd say there are some problems with the idea of health in the first photo because of the danger from the traffic, especially because he's cycling in the night, I mean the dark, and the, um, I can't think of the word, but it's a type of smoke which comes from the cars.

b On the other hand, if you live in the city, it's a good way of getting exercise. In the second photo, the kids should remember that they need to eat a mixed, sorry, a balanced diet, not just salad and fruit.

5 **Answers**
b – Her voice falls at the end of phrases.

5 ▶ Before they start, tell students that they will have exactly a minute to do the task. Time them and say 'Thank you' when the minute is up.

When students have given each other feedback, round up with the whole class and discuss any outstanding points.

CD 2 Track 20

Examiner: In this part of the test, I'm going to give each of you two photographs. I'd like you to talk about your photographs on your own for about a minute, and also to answer a question about your partner's photographs. Student A, here are your photographs. They show people doing healthy activities. I'd like you to compare the photographs and say how important you think each activity is for staying healthy. All right?

6 ▶ Remind students that they should give a relatively short answer to this question – up to 20 seconds.

CD 2 Track 21

Examiner: Student B, which activity would you prefer to do to keep healthy, and why?

7 ▶ Be as strict about timing with this task as in Exercise 5. Round up and discuss feedback at the end.

CD 2 Track 22

Examiner: Now, Student B, here are your photographs. They show two people with minor health problems. I'd like you to compare the photographs and say why it is important for these people to deal with their problems. All right?

8 ▶ Students should also answer this question quite briefly.

CD 2 Track 23

Examiner: Student A, which problem do you think is more serious, and why?

Writing | Part 1 An essay

1 ***As a warmer*** Ask students to look at the photos and say how each of them is connected with health. (Suggested answers: (top left) The photo shows pollution, which has a major effect on people's health, especially their lungs. (top right) Eating four or five pieces of fruit a day is a recommended part of a healthy diet. (bottom left) Our sedentary lifestyle, encouraged by computers, makes people put on weight and become less fit. (bottom right) Taking exercise is good for the body and the mind.)

Alternative treatment The discussion exercise may be fairly lengthy, so if you wish, instead of asking students to change groups and report, you can round up with the whole class by pulling out the main ideas for each discussion point (a–e).

2 ***Alternative treatment*** Since students are familiar with these tasks at this stage in the course, ask them to work alone and then compare their ideas in pairs when they have finished.

> **Suggested underlining**
> Modern lifestyles, endanger, health, food, physical activity

3 ***Alternative treatment*** Elicit the following criteria and write them on the board:

- *Does the essay deal with all parts of the task?*
- *Is the writer's opinion clear?*
- *Are the writer's points supported by reasons and examples?*
- *Does the essay have a clear introduction and conclusion?*
- *Has the writer used linking words and phrases appropriately?*
- *Has the writer used a range of appropriate grammar and written reasonably complex sentences?*
- *Has the writer used a range of appropriate vocabulary?*

Ask students to work through the checklist and point out examples where appropriate.

> **Suggested answers**
> Strong points: It is clearly written in paragraphs, covers the notes in the task and is well linked together.
> Weak points: The writer's opinion is not clear; there is no concluding paragraph.

4 Round up students' ideas with the whole class before moving to Exercise 5.

5
> **Answers**
> **1** c **2** a **3** b

Extension idea Ask students: *Do you agree with the teacher's comments? If not, why not?*

6
> **Answers**
> **1 a** an explanation of healthy aspects of our lifestyles
> **b** things which stop people living healthily
> **2** *However* (contrasts information and ideas with the paragraph before)

7
> **Suggested answers**
> **1** There are three main advantages to living in the country.
> **2** On the other hand, there are several disadvantages to a country life.
> **3** Exercise is important for the following reasons.
> **4** However, there are some dangers attached to taking too much exercise.

8 ***Alternative treatment*** For a change of dynamic, you can do this as a whole-class discussion. However, encourage students to note down a few ideas as they discuss.

9 To give students realistic exam practice, ask them to do this task in 40 minutes.

> **Sample answer**
> Everyone knows that a healthy lifestyle when you are young is essential for staying well as you grow older. However, many young people could do more to look after their health.
> Like everyone else, teenagers should take regular exercise. In my town, perhaps half of the young people I know go running or play football or do some other form of sport, but I have many friends who only do sporting activities occasionally, so they are not really fit. This may be because of the amount of time they have to spend studying.
> On the other hand, it is becoming increasingly common for young people to have a healthy balanced diet, so few people become overweight, which is very important.
> Finally, perhaps because cigarettes are very expensive, few of my friends smoke and this is becoming less fashionable. As a result, I think my generation is healthier than my parents were at my age.
> In conclusion, I believe young people take a reasonable amount of care of themselves although many would benefit from following a regular exercise routine.

12 Animal kingdom

Unit objectives

- **Reading and Use of English Part 1:** revision of words often confused by candidates covered in previous units
- **Reading and Use of English Part 7:** identifying key ideas in questions; attention to tenses and time adverbs
- **Writing Part 2:** writing a letter / an email of advice; ways of giving advice; dealing with content points
- **Listening Part 1:** identifying the main idea in the question; listening for the global meaning
- **Speaking Parts 3 and 4:** dealing with a difficult partner; summarising other people's opinions as well as expressing your own; commenting on the question; expressing agreement/disagreement
- **Pronunciation:** word stress (3)
- **Grammar:** third conditional and mixed conditionals; *wish, if only* and *hope*
- **Vocabulary:** confusion between *avoid, prevent* and *protect; check, control, keep an eye on* and *supervise*; negative prefixes

Starting off

As a warmer Ask students in pairs to look at the photos and describe the role of the animal in each. (Answers: (top left) horse: sport; (top middle) dog: guide dog for the blind; (top right) guinea pig: pet; (middle left) lions (tourism, leisure); (middle right) cow: food (milk); (bottom) camels (transport))

This exercise does not exactly replicate Speaking Part 3, as Speaking Part 3 does not use photo prompts. However, it should provide useful extra practice.

To get students started, elicit the role played by the horse in the first photo. (Suggested answer: For sport and entertainment)

Give students about three minutes for this exercise.

Extension idea To generate some class discussion, ask students: *Which do you think are the most important roles of animals in our lives? Do you think any of the photos show ways in which we should not be using animals? (Why?)*

Listening | Part 1

1 ***As a warmer*** With books closed, ask students in pairs: *What do you know about Listening Part 1? What do you think is good exam advice for Part 1?*

Answers
1 eight; different subjects **2** twice **3** read but don't hear **4** in the question only **5** after you have heard the whole of each piece

2 ▶ Students hear each situation twice, as in the exam.

Extension idea 1 Print out and photocopy the recording script from the Teacher's Resources CD-ROM. Ask students to check their answers and underline the words/phrases which give the answers. They can then compare their ideas in pairs.

Answers
1 C **2** B **3** C **4** B **5** C **6** B **7** A **8** A

Extension idea 2 Ask students: *How do people benefit from keeping pets? Do you think children should have a pet to look after? Why? / Why not? Should people who live in cities keep pets? Why? / Why not?*

CD 2 Track 24

Presenter: One. You overhear a conversation between two women about animals.

Woman 1: My husband is always saying he wishes he had a dog to go for walks with.

Woman 2: So do you think you'll get one?

Woman 1: I don't know. It's such a commitment. I mean, we'd have to take him with us on holiday, that sort of thing, so I'd rule that out. [1]Then my daughter, Patsy, would really like to have a horse.

Woman 2: But that's even more of a commitment!

Woman 1: I know, which is why I hesitate. I mean, we'd have to supervise her quite closely to start with to make sure she was safe. At least until we know she can control it.

Woman 2: What about a cat?

Woman 1: Well, they're definitely the easiest to look after – not that they interest any of us. [1]In the end, we'll probably let Patsy have her choice – it's a mistake to deny your kids the things they really want.

Presenter: Two. You hear part of a television programme about zebras.

Man: To us, every zebra looks alike. During their migration, all the stripes form a confusing pattern which helps to protect them from lions and other predators. But while to the untrained eye they appear identical, each individual's pattern is unique, helping others to identify them. While male zebras have wider, darker, shinier stripes than females, at a distance and in a mass they may all look the same. Even so, [2]young zebras who go off to play can always pick out their mums from thousands of others.

Presenter: Three. You overhear a conversation between a boy and a girl about birds in the girl's garden.

Boy: Hi, Trish. What've you been up to this weekend?

Girl: Oh, I've been helping my mum in the garden a lot of the time.

Boy: So working hard.

Girl: You're telling me! But my mum loves the garden, especially the birds which go there to feed – you know, on insects and berries and things.

Boy: Uh-huh.

Girl: Yeah, and when she's not in the garden, [3]she's watching the birds from the window and keeping an eye out to make sure the cats don't get them. There are tons of cats in our neighbourhood, and she hates the idea of them catching birds. And she's right: dead birds are gross!

Presenter: Four. You overhear part of a conversation in which a girl and a boy are talking about dogs.

Girl: Have you still got that lovely dog of yours?

Boy: We sure have!

Girl: Lucky you! I wish I had a dog.

Boy: Well, he is nice to look at, but we really got him to protect us from burglars. Probably, if we lived in a safer area, we wouldn't have bought one. [4]In fact, he barks at everything, which doesn't make us very popular in the neighbourhood.

Girl: Well, all that barking might prevent a burglary. And I bet he's good fun to play with, isn't he?

Boy: Sure, he's great for that, but I'd be happier if my parents had bought a house in the country. Then we wouldn't worry about neighbours or burglars.

Presenter: Five. You hear a woman giving part of a lecture about animal rights.

Woman: It would, I think, be ignorant to suggest that zoos no longer serve a useful purpose. Many of them do quite valuable work conserving rare species. What I do think, and I'm sure you'd agree with me here, is that those old-fashioned zoos which were designed and built in the 19th century just don't give animals enough space. There's no feeling that animals are in a natural habitat. Those zoos should all be closed and banned, while [5]the more modern zoos need to be strictly inspected to make sure that the animals are kept in the best conditions possible. That way, diseases and other problems can be avoided.

Presenter: Six. You hear a girl talking about some animals she worked with.

Girl: Last summer, you see, I went as a volunteer on a wildlife conservation project in Africa and I was asked to look after these young lions which had been orphaned – you know, they'd lost their mother. It's curious, because I'd expected to feel quite anxious – I mean, they're dangerous animals, aren't they? In fact, [6]after I'd spent a few days feeding the lion cubs and playing with them, we had a very easy, comfortable relationship. I had to keep an eye on them as well, because they could be quite rough when playing with each other, and we didn't want them to harm each other, but I never felt they were going to attack me.

Presenter: Seven. You hear a boy talking about hippos.

Boy: [7]I always thought hippos spent their day hiding in the water, but then I saw this awesome video on YouTube of a guy on holiday in South Africa. It shows him walking along a river bank – he's being filmed by a friend – when suddenly there's this crashing noise in the grass and a hippo rushes out. Wow! Anyway, the guy just manages to leap to one side and run while his mate screams and drops the camera. If he hadn't reacted quickly, the hippo would've killed him, for sure, trampled him underfoot!

Anyway, I got sort of interested in this and Googled 'hippos'. Apparently, they get nervous if someone walks between them and the river, which is their natural habitat, and more people are killed by hippos in Africa every year than by any other animal just because they get between the hippo and the water.

Presenter: Eight. You hear a woman talking to her husband about a circus.

Woman: Brian!

Man: Yes?

Woman: I've been looking in the paper and it's given me an idea. [8]Why don't we take the kids to the circus in the holidays? That's something we haven't done for a few years.

Man: Hmm, I'm not sure. I mean, the last time we went, it wasn't exactly fun, was it?

Woman: Yes, but that's because they had all those acts with tired-looking animals and things. If they'd had more acrobats, we'd have enjoyed it more. Anyway, this one's different. It might be much better.

Man: OK, well, let's ask them if they'd be interested in going.

Vocabulary

avoid, prevent and protect; check, control, keep an eye on and supervise

1 Ask students which situation from Listening Part 1 each extract comes from. Ask who *him* refers to in question 1 (Answer: the dog). Similarly, *they* in question 4 (Answer: lion cubs), *her* and *it* in question 5 (Answers: her daughter and the horse).

After doing question 1, ask: *Which preposition is used with 'protect'?* (Answer: from) (**Note:** *from* is also used with *prevent*, but it is followed by the *-ing* form of the verb, whereas *protect from* is usually followed by a noun.)

Answers
1 supervise; control **2** protect **3** prevent
4 avoided **5** keep an eye on

2 If necessary, go through the dictionary definitions with students. Ask them to refer back to the definitions as they do the exercise.

Answers
1 protecting **2** supervise / keep an eye on
3 control **4** prevents **5** checking **6** avoid
7 protect **8** supervise **9** check **10** control

Extension idea Ask students in pairs to write four sentences using some of the words/phrases from this section. They should gap the words/phrases, then pass their sentences to another pair to complete.

3 **Answers**
1 successfully prevented **2** narrowly avoided
3 properly protected **4** strictly controlled
5 closely supervised **6** avoid; at all costs
6 check; carefully **8** heavily protected

Grammar

Third conditional and mixed conditionals

1 If students are unfamiliar with the third conditional, use these questions and the questions in Exercise 2 to focus on the form (*If* + past perfect, *would have* + past participle) and the meaning (refers to the past, talks about something which did not occur).

Answers
1 T **2** F **3** T

2 When students have done this exercise, go through the notes in the Language reference section on page 165 (Third conditional) with them.

Answers
1 b **2** a **3** b **4** a **5** b **6** a **7** a

3 This exercise concentrates on the form of third conditionals, but if you wish to reinforce the concept, you can ask questions such as (for question 1): *Did Martin concentrate on his work? With what consequence?*

Answers
1 would have finished **2** had known; would have caught **3** would have gone **4** had not been
5 had sat **6** would have enjoyed **7** would not have made **8** would not have heard

4 ***Extension idea*** Tell students to work in pairs and write three more similar questions. They then change partners and take turns to ask their questions and answer their partner's questions. If you do this activity, you will need to monitor carefully that students have the correct form of the questions, i.e. *What would you have done if* + past perfect.

5 Point out the relationship between the second and third conditional, i.e. they both refer to unreal, imaginary, hypothetical situations or events. However, the second conditional refers to present time, while the third conditional refers to past time.

Point out that the first conditional is not possible in mixed-conditional sentences.

Answers
1 **a** second – refers to present time
b third – refers to past time
2 **a** second – refers to present time
b third – refers to past time

6 Remind students that they should look at whether the clause refers to present or past time to decide which conditional to use.

Answers
1 had; would have driven **2** had studied; would not feel / would not be feeling **3** did not bark; would have taken **4** had not been; would still be

7 **Answers**
1 would have allowed him **2** had left home earlier **3** less frightening; I would have **4** had spoken more slowly

Extension idea Ask students to think of three things which happened in the past which have made their lives different now – you might elicit one or two examples, e.g. *If my mother hadn't changed her job, I wouldn't live in this city.*

They then work in small groups and take turns to tell each other what happened and how their lives are different, using mixed conditionals.

This would be a suitable moment to do the photocopiable activity on the Teacher's Resources CD-ROM.

Reading and Use of English | Part 1

1 ***As a warmer*** Ask students: *Did you go to circuses when you were younger? If so, what animals did you see? What did the animals do? Did you enjoy seeing animals in circuses?*

2 **Answers**
1 eight **2** the text quickly **3** after **4** the options **5** you have finished **6** all the questions

3 **Answers**
horses

4 ***As a warmer*** Elicit why C (*own*) is the correct answer in question 0. Elicit that for A we say *The circus belongs to them*, and B and D have the wrong meanings.

Answers
1 A **2** C **3** D **4** B **5** D **6** A **7** D **8** C

5 ***Alternative treatment*** Tell students they will debate these questions. Divide the class into two groups and ask one group to brainstorm reasons why using or keeping animals in circuses and zoos is cruel. Ask the other group to brainstorm reasons why it is OK. Then divide them into groups of approximately six (with three for and three against) to debate the question.

Grammar

wish, if only and *hope*

1 Point out that *if only* is an emphatic way of saying *I wish*, but that its grammar is the same.

Answers
1 a, b, d and e **2** a, b and d **3** b **4** past tense and *would* + infinitive **5** c **6** past perfect **7** f **8** present simple

2 Before doing this exercise, go through the notes in the Language reference section on page 180 (*wish, if only* and *hope*) with your students.

Answers
1 ~~wish~~ hope **2** ~~wish~~ hope **3** correct **4** ~~wish~~ hope **5** correct **6** ~~wish~~ hope **7** correct **8** ~~wish~~ hope

Extension idea Ask students to write five sentences which are true for themselves using *wish*, *if only* and *hope*. Encourage them to use different tenses to show they know how to use the patterns. They should then work in small groups and read out their sentences to their group.

Alternatively, they can walk around the class to find someone else who has the most similar wishes and hopes to them.

3 To help students get started, for question 1, elicit that in the question *cook* is a verb, but that in the answer it is a noun.

Answers
1 was a better **2** I'd / I had studied harder **3** would make less OR wouldn't / would not make so much **4** hadn't / had not called off **5** wish you'd / you had met

Reading and Use of English | Part 7

1 ***As a warmer*** With books closed, ask students in pairs: *What do you remember about Reading and Use of English Part 7 – what does it consist of, and how do you do it?*

They then do the exercise in the book.

Answers
1 F (There are ten.) **2** T **3** F (Read the questions carefully first.) **4** T **5** F (Answer all the questions.)

2 Ask also: *Have you ever seen any of these animals? If so, where?*

3 ***Alternative treatment (Exercises 3 and 4)*** To make the reading task communicative, ask students to

work in pairs or small groups, making sure there is an even number of pairs / small groups.

Tell them they are either A or B. Those who are A should answer questions 1, 3, 5, 7 and 9. Those who are B should answer questions 2, 4, 6, 8 and 10.

Give them a time limit of ten minutes to underline the key ideas in their questions, answer them and check their answers with their partners.

When they have finished, ask students to form new pairs consisting of a Student A and a Student B. They should then exchange answers and explain why they chose that answer.

Suggested underlining
1 didn't immediately realise, injured **2** unwilling, injure, animal **3** believes, behaviour caused, attack **4** advice, ignored **5** people, lacked, knowledge to help **6** considered, missed, opportunity **7** regrets, result, encounter **8** might not have been injured, another time **9** happy at first, animal, attacked **10** surprised, eventually escape

4 ***Alternative treatment*** (if you did not do the one in Exercise 3 above)

Ask students to work in pairs and read one of the extracts only.

They then match the questions which correspond to that extract and make sure that they both understand the extract.

Ask them to form new groups of four with students who have read other extracts.

Students then take turns to tell the story of their extract and explain which questions correspond with their extract, and why.

If their answers overlap in any cases, they can then discuss and solve the questions together.

Answers
1 B **2** C **3** D **4** A **5** B **6** B **7** D **8** B **9** D **10** A

5 Students should answer using third conditional sentences.

When they have finished, round up ideas with the whole class.

Speaking | Parts 3 and 4

As a warmer Ask: *How are Speaking Parts 3 and 4 connected?* (Answer: The questions in Part 4 will be on topics related to Part 3.)

1 Tell students that in the first part of this Speaking section, they are going to hear two students doing the same Part 3 twice. The first time, they will hear what happens when things go wrong.

Give them a few moments to look at the task before you play the recording.

After they have listened, elicit that part of the problem is that a) Miguel is a very competent speaker, and b) he has not realised that this is a collaborative task. This sort of problem may arise in the exam when the two candidates do not know each other and when a candidate who may be a competent speaker has not done an exam preparation course and is therefore unaware of what is expected and is not paying careful attention to the instructions.

Point out that in the exam itself, neither candidate would necessarily be penalised. In the event of one candidate speaking much more than the other in Part 3, the examiner will rebalance the situation by asking the other candidate more questions in Part 4.

Answers
1 Miguel is doing all the speaking and not giving Irene a chance to participate.
2 *Suggested answer:* Irene needs to find an opportunity to interrupt.

CD 2 Track 25

Examiner: Now I'd like you to talk about something together for about two minutes. I'd like you to imagine that a famous animal expert has offered to give a talk to students at your school about some aspect of animals and the natural world. Here are some of the subjects he has said he can talk about and a question for you to discuss. First, you have some time to look at the task. Now talk to each other about what students would find interesting and useful about each of these subjects.

Miguel: I think choosing a pet could be interesting and useful for students who are thinking of adopting a cat or a dog or some other animal to share their home, so they can find the right one, or one that suits them and not one which is going to give them problems. And the talk about animals in danger is important for learning to look after the environment so that animals don't become extinct or disappear. But on the other hand, we see this sort of subject on television all the time and for students it might not be too interesting. Also, I suppose if there are students who are thinking of becoming farmers or vets, then working with animals might be quite interesting, though it wouldn't really interest me …

2 Tell students that they are unlikely to have such an extreme situation as in Exercise 1 and that small discreet interruptions like Irene's are likely to be enough.

Point out that, by agreeing, she is making the interruption less aggressive and so she is less likely to upset Miguel.

Answers
Yes, I agree, and; Yes, you're right, but

CD 2 Track 26

Miguel: I think choosing a pet could be interesting and useful for students who are thinking of adopting a cat or a dog or some other animal to share their home, so they can find the right one, or one which suits them–

Irene: Yes, I agree, and, and it will help them to learn a bit about what common pets are like, you know, er, their characteristics and perhaps a bit about how to look after them properly as well.

Miguel: And the subject of animals in danger is important for learning to look after the environment so that animals don't become extinct or disappear. It will make students more aware of the problem–

Irene: Yes, you're right, but, but we see this sort of thing on television all the time, so unless he has something new or unusual to say, this might be a subject students already know quite a lot about …

3 Give students two minutes to do this task. Round up by asking them how successful they were at interrupting.

4 Give students one minute to do this task.

CD 2 Track 27

Examiner: Now you have about a minute to decide which two subjects it would be best for the expert to speak about.

Extension idea Round up by asking different pairs what they decided, and why.

5 ***Alternative treatment*** Play the recording twice. The first time, students should note down the questions the examiner asks (see the recording script for Track 28). The second time, they should answer question 1. When they have done all parts of this exercise, ask them to take turns to ask and answer the questions themselves.

Answers
1 c
2 **comment on the question:** That's a difficult question; That's quite interesting
introduce other people's opinions: People often suggest that …; Some people say that …
say whether you agree or disagree with other people's opinions: I think that's true; I'm not sure that I agree

CD 2 Track 28

Examiner: Irene, do you think animals should be kept in zoos?

Irene: That's a difficult question. Some people say that it's cruel to keep animals in zoos where they don't have the freedom that they'd have in their natural habitat. They say that animals get stressed and can't relax, but I'm not sure that I agree. I think they can. If animals have some space, they can have a nice relaxed life in a zoo because no other animals will attack them, and they don't have to look for food either.

Examiner: And what can children learn from keeping animals at home as pets?

Irene: That's quite interesting. People often suggest that children learn to be responsible because they have to look after the animal. I think that's true and also, from my experience, I think it's an extra relationship which develops children's ability to love and care about the animals and the people around them.

Examiner: And Miguel, what can people learn from watching programmes about animals on television?

7 Also encourage students to comment on the question before they answer it – though you can tell them that they certainly do not always have to do so, only when they genuinely would like to comment.

6 Pronunciation: word stress (3)

This pronunciation section works on using /ə/ in unstressed grammar words.

1 ▶

> **Answers**
> See recording script for Track 29.

CD 2 Track 29

That's a difficult question. Some people say that it's cruel to keep animals in zoos where they don't have the freedom that they'd have in their natural habitat.

They say that animals get stressed and can't relax, but I'm not sure that I agree. I think they can. If animals have some space, they can have a nice relaxed life in a zoo …

That's quite interesting. People often suggest that children learn to be responsible because they have to look after the animal.

I think that's true and also, from my experience, I think that it's an extra relationship which develops children's ability to love and care about the animals and the people around them.

2 ***Extension idea*** Write *that, some, can* and *and* on the board. Read each of them aloud in their stressed and unstressed form, asking students to repeat after you.

3 ***Alternative treatment*** Ask students in pairs to take turns reading the sentences. The student who is listening should chip in on the highlighted words when they are stressed, e.g.

Student 1: That's a difficult question. Some people say that it's cruel to keep …

Student 2: That's .... Some ....

4 ▶ ***Extension idea*** Ask: *How does the meaning of the sentence change when the highlighted words are stressed?* (Suggested answers: **a** emphasing that both things are required, not just time; **b** emphasising how she got to the station; **c** suggesting that he is not now; **d** emphasising the question about where the person was – not in the place we previously supposed; **e** emphasising the fact that it is a possibility, i.e. that they are not always noisy.)

CD 2 Track 30

See page 136 of the Student's Book.

Writing | Part 2 A letter or email

1 ***As a warmer*** With books closed, ask students in pairs: *If you were visiting Britain for the first time, what advice would you ask for from a British friend before going?* You can suggest areas such as accommodation, driving on the left, food, etc.

With books open, point out the difference in spelling between *advice* and *advise* (Answer: *advise* – verb; *advice* – noun).

> **Suggested answers**
> **1** where to go, what to see and the best way of getting around to see countryside, scenery and wildlife
> **3** informal style – it's a letter to a friend – he has written to you in an informal style.

2 When students have written their plans, ask them to change partners and compare their ideas.

3
> **Answers**
> **1** I'm very glad to hear that you're thinking of visiting my country this summer. **2** yes – advice about visiting Asturias, what to see while there, and hiring a car **3** yes – he adds information **4** quite informal

Extension idea Ask students to compare their plans with Manolo's letter. Does it deal with things in the same way or differently?

4
> **Answers**
> **1** I'd advise you to go to Asturias **2** You should visit the 'Picos de Europa' **3** If I were you, I'd hire a car to get around. **4** The best idea would be to hire it online **5** Make sure that you take warm clothes and a raincoat

5 ***Alternative treatment*** As a light-hearted activity, ask students to think of 'wrong' advice which they could give foreign visitors which might get them into trouble, e.g. 'Public buildings are kept very clean, so make sure you always take your shoes off before entering them.'

6 If you decide to give this task for homework, tell students that in the exam, they would have about 40 minutes for it.

→ For more on writing emails and letters, you can refer students to page 189 (Writing reference – Emails and letters).

> **Sample answer**
> See the model letter in Exercise 3.

Vocabulary and grammar review Unit 11

1 **1** diagnosed **2** heal **3** treatment **4** infection **5** put on **6** fit **7** prescription **8** cure **9** check-up **10** get over

2 **1** misunderstood **2** disapprove **3** dissatisfied **4** inexperienced **5** dislikes **6** unwilling **7** unnatural **8** misleading **9** unfashionable **10** unacceptable **11** unreliable **12** dishonest

3 **1** whose arm is broken has **2** one the injury (which/that) / the one (which/that) the **3** whose inhabitants are (all) **4** in a/the way (that/which) **5** from his email what **6** (which/that) Chiaro tells do not / don't

Vocabulary and grammar review Unit 12

1 **1** B **2** C **3** A **4** D **5** A **6** B

2 **1** had not / hadn't been **2** was/were **3** wasn't/ weren't; would have had **4** would not / wouldn't make **5** lived **6** has not / hasn't missed **7** would speak **8** would be **9** will change / are going to change **10** had studied **11** would have got **12** had eaten

3 **1** had not / hadn't left **2** had paid her in **3** have made a/any difference **4** had a better relationship with **5** would help him once in **6** had not / hadn't turned him down

13 House space

Unit objectives

- **Reading and Use of English Part 5:** practice in skimming; work on references and inferencing
- **Reading and Use of English Part 2:** skimming the text
- **Writing Part 2:** writing an article describing your ideal home; analysing the task
- **Listening Part 2:** predicting the type of information and types of words needed
- **Speaking Part 2:** comparing places to live; speculating about what it would be like to live there; concentrating on dealing with the question
- **Pronunciation:** linking (2)
- **Grammar:** causative *have* and *get*; expressing obligation and permission
- **Vocabulary:** types of home; confusion between *space, place, room, area, location* and *square*; collocations with *area, place, room* and *space*; vocabulary for house maintenance; words and phrases to describe places to live, e.g. *close to nature, environment,* etc.

Starting off

1 ***As a warmer*** With book closed, ask students in small groups:

- *If you could choose anywhere in the world to live, where would you live, and in what type of house?*
- *What are the most important things when deciding where to live, e.g. a safe neighbourhood, being near the place where you work or study, etc.?*

Students then open their books and do the exercise.

Answers
1 c **2** b **3** a **4** d **5** f **6** e

2 Encourage students to give reasons for their opinions.

Extension idea Ask students what other facilities they think would be important.

3 Groups of three or four would be ideal. Tell them that they should discuss each of the options and try to reach agreement. This activity is similar to Speaking Part 3.

Reading and Use of English | Part 5

1 ***As a warmer*** Ask students what they know about Venice. Ask them if they think it would be a good place to live. You can ask about getting about by canal (perhaps not having a car), climate (it may be damp), numbers of tourists, etc. Students then do the exercise in the book.

2 ***Alternative treatment*** With books closed, ask students to work in small groups and brainstorm what they remember about Reading and Use of English Part 5. They then check by doing the Exam round-up.

Answers
1 six **2** the text quickly before reading the questions **3** after

3 Give students two minutes to do this.

Suggested answer
It's conveniently situated close to the Grand Canal, the district is interesting, it's near the city centre and easy for clients to find, the printing trade has many roots in the area.

4 If necessary, remind students to underline the key idea in the question, then to find and read the relevant section of the text before they read the options.

Answers
1 C **2** B **3** C **4** D **5** D **6** A

5 Before they start, you can suggest possible places: somewhere they have spent a holiday, a friend's house, their grandparents' house, etc. Suggest things they can say, e.g. where the house is, what sort of house it is, what the neighbourhood is like, what they enjoy doing there, etc.

Vocabulary

space, place, room, area, location and *square*

1 

Answers
1 place **2** square **3** location **4** area

2 Tell students they should pay special attention when they use these words. If they notice they have made a mistake, they should correct it.

Answers
1 space **2** room **3** space **4** location **5** area **6** space **7** square **8** area **9** space **10** room

Extension idea Ask students to write their own sentences using each of the words.

3 Point out to students that, as collocations, these combinations are not exclusive or fixed, for example *hiding space* and *meeting room* are also collocations.

To help students, you can print and photocopy the word list from the Teacher's Resources CD-ROM, which contains some of the less obvious of these collocational phrases.

Answers
1 place **2** space **3** room **4** area

4

Answers
1 parking spaces **2** personal space **3** green space **4** legroom / leg room **5** market place **6** picnic area

Extension idea Ask students in pairs to write four more sentences with the collocational phrases gapped. They then pass them to another pair, who have to complete the sentences.

Listening | Part 2

1 ***As a warmer*** Ask students: *Which would you prefer: to live in a typical modern house, or an old historic house? Why?* Then move to the question in the book.

2

Answers
1 F – You hear a talk given by one person. **2** F – It has ten questions. **3** F – You will need between one and three words. **4** T **5** T **6** F – You should read and try to predict the type of information and type of words you need. **7** T

3 ***Alternative treatment***

Ask students to work in pairs and tell them they are competing with the rest of the class.

Tell them to actually predict the answers, i.e. they write a plausible answer in each gap.

They compare and discuss their predictions with another pair, then do the listening exercise.

The winning pair is the pair with the most correct predictions.

Suggested answers
2 probably a noun **3** a person **4** name of a room **5** probably a verb / verb phrase **6** another type of room **7** another type of building / something that was there before **8** a machine or other facility **9** a noun **10** an adverb

4 Play the recording twice, as in the exam.

Give students time to check their answers. Then ask them to work in pairs and compare their answers.

If you wish, print out and photocopy the recording script from the Teacher's Resources CD-ROM for them to check their answers while you play the recording a third time.

Answers
1 eight/8 years **2** (strange) experiences **3** uncle **4** kitchen **5** (standing) behind **6** (old) garage **7** battle **8** tennis court **9** blood **10** at weekends

CD 2 Track 31

Jeff: Hi, so as part of our project on historic local buildings, I thought I'd tell you about the house where I live. My mum and dad bought it when I was about seven, so we've been there for about [1]eight years now. It isn't all that old – it was built about 15 years ago – but it's on the site of a much older place dating back to the 15th century which fell down. Anyway, why I'm telling you all this is 'cos we're pretty sure the house is haunted – I mean, it's got ghosts. Yeah, you can laugh, but I'm not joking. I know 'cos I know several people, myself included, who've had some [2]strange experiences there. Yeah, yeah, you may think I'm just telling you a story, but a couple of years ago I remember, my mum and dad had invited all sorts of relatives to one of those big family celebrations and we were all sitting round after lunch – I was playing some game with my cousins, and my grandma was telling everyone about her visits to the doctor or something, when my [3]uncle suddenly went pale and dropped his coffee cup. Grandma thought he'd been taken ill or something 'cos of her stories, but he said he'd just seen a group of men dressed up as medieval soldiers go past the window. We cousins ran outside to take a look, but there was nobody there. Anyway, when he'd calmed down, he described their appearance in quite a lot of detail, so he wasn't just making it up. Then, a couple of months later, a friend of my mum's was staying with us. My mum was busy in her study and I was watching football on the telly in the sitting room when the friend came rushing out of the [4]kitchen shouting and hollering that he'd seen the table sort of float across the room. I've never seen a grown-up tremble like he did, so when we went to look, the table had actually moved and it's one of those really heavy old oak ones. It took three of us to push it back, so he couldn't have done it on his own. Anyway, I'm not sure if it's because of the things which've happened, but when I'm studying in my room, I sometimes feel as if there's someone [5]standing behind me, sort of breathing down my neck and checking what I'm doing like it's one of my teachers – I mean, I can feel the breath – but when I turn round, there's no one there. That shakes me up a bit! Anyway, my mum complained that she was experiencing the same thing, so she got the builders in and she had the [6]old garage at the back of the house turned into a study so she could work there instead without being interrupted by these uninvited visitors! Then my dad got the whole house checked by a specialist in supernatural phenomena, a sort of ghost hunter. She checked local history records and apparently the house is actually located somewhere where, after one of those invasions, a [7]battle took place a few hundred years ago with lots of fighting, so there could be quite a few bodies buried there. Weird, isn't it? A bit later, my dad decided to have a [8]tennis court built in a corner of the garden, so he and I could play together. Anyway, one of the workers was on his own there one morning when he felt someone watching him. When he turned round, he saw something which literally made his hair stand on end: a man standing there with a white shirt covered in [9]blood. The lad shouted and the man just disappeared. When we questioned him – you know, he was gibbering and shaking – he didn't know anything about the other supernatural experiences people had been having. My mum's getting a bit fed up with all these happenings, but my dad doesn't mind them so much. You see, he's only down here [10]at weekends 'cos he works in London during the week.

5 ***Extension idea*** Ask students if they know the history of the house they live in, e.g. when the house was built, who built it, who lived in it before, etc. Ask them to tell their partners what they know.

Grammar

Causative *have* and *get*

1 **Answers**
His mother had the garage converted into a study, and his father had a tennis court built.

2 When students have answered the questions, go through the notes in the Language reference section on page 164 (Causative *have* and *get*) with them.

Answers
1 b
2 a – He/She did it himself/herself; b – He/She asked someone else to do it for them
3 Other people – an architect and/or builders (1); a ghost hunter (2)

3 **Answers**
1 to have/get (your passport) renewed **2** had/got (a tooth) pulled out **3** having/getting (the house) painted **4** have/get (it) cut down **5** have/get (it) extended **6** has/gets (all his meals) delivered

Extension idea Ask students to say or write down three things they have had done recently. They then work in pairs and their partners ask them *yes/no* questions to find out what they were.

4 **Answers**
1 had my bag stolen while **2** is having/getting his picture taken **3** have/get her hair dyed **4** his application turned down

Reading and Use of English | Part 2

1 You can ask students if they think living on a houseboat is cheaper or more expensive, safer or more dangerous, more convenient or less convenient, more comfortable or less comfortable, etc.

2 Before doing the Exam round-up, with books closed, ask students how they should go about doing the task.

Answers
1 eight **2** grammar **3** general idea **4** before and after **5** one word ONLY **6** the completed text

3 Students can answer this question in pairs.

4 When students have finished, ask them to work in pairs or small groups to compare their ideas before going through the answers with them.

Answers
1 as **2** spite **3** since **4** hardly **5** According **6** takes **7** out **8** come/pop

5 ***Extension idea*** You can follow up these questions with questions such as:

- *What do you enjoy doing when friends visit you?*
- *How do you entertain visitors in your home in your country?* etc.

Speaking | Part 2

1 ***As a warmer*** With books closed, ask students what they remember about Speaking Part 2. You can ask questions such as these:

- *Do you do this part of the exam in pairs, or do you work alone?* (Answer: Alone)
- *Do you have to talk about photos, or just answer a question?* (Answer: You have to do both.)
- *How long do you have to speak for?* (Answer: About a minute) etc.

Then ask them to answer the questions in the Exam round-up box.

Answers
1 T **2** F – two photos **3** F – compare the main ideas and discuss the question **4** T **5** T

2 Ask students to note down their ideas. Then round up with the whole class and write useful vocabulary on the board for them to copy into their notebooks.

3 ***Alternative treatment*** Print out and photocopy the word list from the Teacher's Resources CD-ROM so that students can check the definitions of some of these words and phrases where necessary.

Suggested answers
Photo 1: close to nature, fresh air, organic food, a rural setting
Photo 2: hi-tech, sophisticated entertainment, pollution
Both photos: environment, maintain a lifestyle, occupants, spend quality time, social life

4 Tell students they do not have to use all the words/ phrases from Exercises 2 and 3, but these are a resource if they need them.

Check the time they start speaking and say 'Thank you' at the end of a minute.

5 ***Alternative treatment*** Before they listen, ask students in pairs to look at the checklist and say which are good things to aim to do in Speaking Part 2. (Suggested answer: 2, 3, 4, 5, 6, 7)

Answers
1 F **2** T **3** T **4** T **5** T **6** T **7** T **8** F **9** F

CD 2 Track 32

Examiner: Peter, it's your turn first. Here are your photographs. They show two different places to live. I'd like you to compare the photographs and say what you think it is like for the people to live in each of these places. All right?

Peter: OK. The first photo shows a traditional country cottage with the occupants, a family, standing in the garden where they grow their own vegetables, whereas the second photo shows a young family living in a smart luxury flat with a view of the city. I guess both photos show a lifestyle which the people have chosen and which they like, so for both families, it must be very pleasant to live where they do. Living in the country cottage must be very peaceful, with very little stress, no pollution and plenty of physical work, healthy organic food and fresh air. On the other hand, living in the city flat might be quite exciting because you're at the centre of things, with entertainment and friends close by. I think the first photo shows a way of life where money and success in your career are not so important as being close to nature and the countryside. The people living in this sort of environment probably have plenty of time to spend together. The family in the second photo must need to earn quite a lot of money to maintain their lifestyle, which is probably busier and more stressful.

Examiner: Thank you. Martyna, which place would you choose to live in?

Martyna: I'd choose the city flat because I can only fulfil my ambitions in a city, so I'd have to live there as well.

Examiner: Thank you. Now, here are your photographs. They show …

6 **Pronunciation:** linking (2)

1 Remind students that they worked on linking words which end and begin with consonant sounds in Unit 10.

Answers
a y [j] **b** r [r] **c** w [w]

CD 2 Track 33

a … with the occupants, a family, standing in the garden. On the other hand, living in the city flat might be quite exciting.

b … where they grow their own vegetables.
… money and success in your career are not so important as being close to nature and the countryside.
… which is probably busier and more stressful.

c ... money and success in your career are not so important.
The family in the second photo must need to earn quite a lot of money.

2 While their partner is reading, students should listen and say if they have heard the linking consonant.

3 

Answers
1 further-r-away; the-y-old **2** he-y-ever-r-answer **3** Our-r-aunt; stay-y-at; now-w-and **4** fewer-r-and; our-r-area are-r-open **5** Many-y-of; busy-y-and **6** The-y-end; more-r-exciting

CD 2 Track 34

See page 146 of the Student's Book.

4 Ask students to slightly exaggerate the consonant link. Follow up by asking them if they find using the consonant makes it easier to pronounce the sentences.

5 ***Alternative treatment*** As students are working in pairs, after each student has read a sentence, tell the student who is listening to say whether they agree or disagree with what their partner has just said, and why.

Tell them that as they speak, they should spontaneously try to use the linking they have been practising.

7 ***Alternative treatment*** Before they start, ask students in pairs to look back at other Speaking sections where they have worked on Speaking Part 2. Tell them you would like them to find strategies and ways of dealing with the task which would be really worth remembering for the exam. (They practised Speaking Part 2 in Units 2, 6, 9 and 11.)

Give them some time to do this and then round up ideas with the whole class. Write them on the board for students to bear in mind.

8 After students have given feedback, round up the main points with the whole class.

Grammar

Expressing obligation and permission

1 ***As a warmer*** If appropriate, ask students if they have ever stayed with a host family, or had a student staying with them. What was the experience like?

2 **Answers**
1 a I have to **b** I can't; they won't let me **c** I can; They let me **2** b

3 

Answers
1 Miguel: D **2** Irene: E **3** Martyna: C **4** Nikolai: B **5** Antonia: A

Extension idea Ask students: *Whose host family sounds the nicest? Would you enjoy having a student staying in your house?*

CD 2 Track 35

Antonia: So, what's your host family like, Miguel? Are they friendly?

Miguel: Yeah, they're great fun, especially the mum. She's always cracking jokes and suggesting interesting things to do. And she's got a couple of daughters my age who don't stop laughing! The house is always full of their friends too, so it's like a permanent party, and that's great for my social life. The only drawback is that [1]<u>I can't stay out too late</u> because they all have to be up early the next morning. I don't have to do anything around the house or things like that – though I do help from time to time, just to fit in and make things easier for them. What about you, Irene?

Irene: You sound really lucky with your family, Miguel. Mind you, I haven't got any complaints, but my family certainly isn't as much fun as yours. I mean, they didn't let me invite a couple of friends to dinner the other day. They told me it just wasn't convenient and I can see that's not being unreasonable, it is their house after all. And anyway, it's not always like that – for example, the other day when I wanted to go down to the seaside for the day, [2]<u>they actually lent me their car</u>. I thought that was really nice of them and very trusting. I mean, I've only just passed my test! Are you living with a nice family, Martyna?

Martyna: Well, we have our ups and downs. The other day, my landlady told me off because I'd got home a bit late and missed the family dinner. Apparently, I was supposed to phone to say I wasn't coming. Then when [3]<u>I went to see if there was anything left over in the fridge</u>, I got into trouble again. <u>She told me I couldn't just help myself to things</u> without asking her first.

Miguel: So, what did you do? Walk out?

Martyna: No, I apologised for being late and explained that I had to finish some project work at school. She calmed down and said 'Never mind,' and then she helped me to cook myself a really nice meal. So we were all friends again.

Nikolai: Great. Still, all your families sound really nice to me.

Martyna: And isn't yours, Nikolai?

Nikolai: Well, they're all right, I suppose. Not very tidy, which is one thing I would complain about. I'm not the tidiest person myself, but I think they're just taking advantage of homestay students by saying that [4]anyone staying in their home must do their share around the house – you know, like clearing up a bit, doing a bit of the hoovering, a bit of the cooking. I needn't clean the bathroom or do any shopping, fortunately, because I wouldn't have the time. But I doubt if they'd let me have my friends in for dinner or anything like that. Not like you, Antonia.

Antonia: Well, I'm lucky. [5]Martyna, you've been round for dinner and so has Nikolai. I had to buy the food and cook it of course and they don't allow me to have big parties, but a couple of friends is OK. And they join in too, which makes it really interesting because we have – I don't know, like a sort of international evening. It's quite good fun. And I cook traditional Sicilian food, which makes a change for everyone.

Miguel: It sounds as if we're all quite lucky, then. Not like a friend of mine who went back to Peru last year ...

4 **Answers**
1 Miguel **2** Antonia **3** Antonia **4** Martyna
5 Irene **6** Nikolai

5 When students have completed the table, go through the Language reference section on page 171 (Expressing obligation, prohibition and permission) with them.

Answers
obligation (present): I must, I'm supposed to, I have to
obligation (past): I had to, I was supposed to
prohibition (present): I can't, I'm not allowed to, They won't let me, They don't allow me to
prohibition (past): They didn't let me
permission (present): I can, They let me
no obligation (present): I don't have to, I needn't

6 **Answers**
1 not allow him **2** do not have to **3** am supposed to take **4** are not allowed (to go) **5** to let Celia borrow **6** not let us use

This would be a suitable moment to do the photocopiable activity for this unit from the Teacher's Resources CD-ROM.

Writing | Part 2 An article

1 **Answers**
a 6 **b** 4 **c** 1 **d** 3 **e** 2 **f** 5

2 Here, you can encourage students to be as extravagant as they wish – they are not limited by money. Encourage them to recycle vocabulary from the unit.

3 Ask students to speak for about a minute. This will help their timing for Part 2 of the Speaking paper.

4 **Suggested answers**
1 readers of the college magazine, i.e. other students, teachers, etc. **2** informal **3** conditional – it asks you to imagine your ideal home **4** the type of house, its location and features of the house **5** for example, by surprising the reader, by saying interesting things about yourself

5 **Answers**
2 Yes – type of house: small, stylish, modern flat; location: Barcelona or Bologna, conveniently close to cafes, art galleries and shops; features: cosy bedroom, handy kitchen, balcony, etc.

6 **Suggested answers**
Para. 1: Type of flat and location; my present accommodation; advantages of ideal flat
Para. 2: Characteristics of flat
Para. 3: Conclusion: room for my things

7 **Answers**
1 from **2** where **3** own **4** what/whatever/anything **5** have **6** few **7** long **8** If

8 **Answers**
1 T **2** T **3** F **4** T (She would like to live alone and make her own decisions, she enjoys art and reading, she wants an active social life.) **5** T
6 F (She lives in a small suburban house.)

9 If you give the task for homework, tell students that in the exam, they would have 40 minutes for it.

→ For more on writing articles, you can refer students to page 193 (Writing reference – Articles).

Sample answer
See the model answer in Exercise 5.

14 Fiesta!

Unit objectives

- **Reading and Use of English Part 6:** round-up of reading techniques for this task, including noting the text structure; use of referencing and cohesive features
- **Reading and Use of English Part 3:** forming personal nouns; identifying the type of word needed
- **Writing Part 1:** writing an essay discussing advantages and disadvantages; using commas; referencing using pronominal *it, this, that* and *they*
- **Listening Part 4:** identifying key ideas; listening for gist and detail
- **Speaking Parts 3 and 4:** supporting and encouraging your partner
- **Pronunciation:** improving fluency
- **Grammar:** the passive; patterns after passive reporting verbs, i.e. *that* + clause or infinitive
- **Vocabulary:** activities and collocations for festivals and celebrations; *celebrate, commemorate, hold street parties,* etc.; features of festivals; suffixes to form personal nouns

Starting off

1 *As a warmer* Before they open their books, ask students to work in small groups and say what events are typical for public festivals and celebrations in their country. When are the most important festivals? Then move on to the exercise in the book.

Answers
1 celebrate **2** dress up; perform **3** march; commemorate **4** hold **5** play/perform **6** gather round **7** let off **8** wearing

2 **Answers**
Photos: 1 traditional costumes, parade **2** fireworks **3** traditional costumes, traditional dances **4** street parties **5** parade, bands, traditional costumes **6** disguises, traditional costumes **7** street performers

Extension idea Ask students to suggest other photos which could be included with these ones.

3 Give students about three minutes to do this.

4 ***Alternative treatment*** Ask students to work alone first and prepare a short talk to answer this question. If they wish, they can use dictionaries or the internet (if available) to prepare what they want to say. Allow them to make notes. They then give their talk to a partner or to the rest of the class.

Listening | Part 4

1 Tell students you are not going to help them with vocabulary for the first question – if they do not know the exact word, they need to find ways to explain what they mean using other words.

Suggested answers
fire-eating, sword-swallowing, acrobatics, clowning and comedy, singing and dancing, etc.

A possible follow-up question: *Why do you think people become street performers?*

2 **Answers**
1 an interview **2** seven **3** underline; different words **4** general ideas

3 If necessary, remind students to underline the key ideas as they read the questions.

Answers
1 C **2** A **3** B **4** A **5** B **6** A **7** C

CD 2 Track 36

Interviewer: Today, *South Live* visits the Winchester Hat Fair, an extravaganza of processions, fireworks and street theatre with performers from as far away as Australia and Brazil. And we're talking to a veteran performer at the Hat Fair, Mighty Max, who's come all the way from Canada once again. Max, why's the festival called the Hat Fair?

Max: Well, I've been told the fair was only started in 1974, as a way of encouraging street performers like myself. It's not like there was one of those great old English traditions like hat-making here in the 18th century or anything. Lots of people come to the fair wearing funny hats because of the name, but that wasn't its origins. [1]It was always supposed to be about street theatre, and during the act, a hat's passed around so that the performers can earn a living. And that, in fact's where the name comes from.

Interviewer: Now, you've been coming here for a number of years. Why do you keep coming back?

Max: Oh, I just love performing here. There are artists like myself from all over the world who come here year after year and we get to know each other and stuff. [2]But what makes the fair unique is the people who come to watch. You know, you jump around and do your act and they really let their hair down and love it when they're being made a fool of by other people in the crowd, and [2]that's really what makes it such fun.

Interviewer: So, how did you get involved in street theatre in the first place?

Max: Well, you know, my big ambition was to be a circus performer. I actually went to quite a famous circus school in Canada as a teenager where I was taught juggling and acrobatics. My dad was dead against it, but he paid for the classes on the condition that I went to university and got myself what he called 'a proper education' as well. It was ironic, really, because [3]if I hadn't gone to university, I might never have got into street theatre. You see, [3]every vacation I had time to travel and I found I could pay for my trips by performing in the street and making a collection.

Interviewer: Fantastic! Your act's been attracting tremendous crowds here in Winchester. How do you explain your popularity?

Max: Well, it's a combination of high-class acrobatics, which are performed without any safety equipment at all, and some quite risky stunts. So it gives the audience a thrill – you know, there are plenty of oohs and aahs, but [4]what I think really gets them into it is that I make them laugh. There's a lot of clowning in my act, which builds a sort of two-way communication with the audience, and they love it.

Interviewer: The acts I've seen around town today have been pretty high quality. Why do you think that is?

Max: Well, there's plenty of money around this town, which certainly attracts the best people from around the world, but you know, [5]none of that money's going to go in the hat unless your act is a good one, and so you've gotta make sure people have a really great time watching you work.

Interviewer: And what difficulties do street performers come up against?

Max: Good question. In a place like Winchester, not many. We're each given a place and a time to perform. As you've seen, I attract pretty large crowds and I need plenty of space, so narrow streets are no good. Here, we're given the main shopping street, which is fine. In other places, if you haven't got permission, you'll get moved on by the police, so I always make sure that I've got the right permits. Actually, [6]what's most likely to stop things happening the way you'd like is usually the rain or even just a bit of drizzle. I mean, where's the fun in standing around getting cold and wet?

Interviewer: None at all. But what about Winchester? Has the Hat Fair put the town on the map? I mean, does it attract a lot of visitors from outside?

Max: I'm not the best person to answer that question. I get the impression that the people who come here tend to be from the surrounding area rather than tourists. What Winchester gets is an amusing party – something they can do which is just plain fun. [7]They gather in the streets and parks and unwind and forget about the other stuff in their lives.

Interviewer: Mighty Max, thank you, and I hope the rest of the fair goes well for you.

Max: Thank you.

4 **Suggested answers**
Some residents may find it annoying or noisy, it interrupts traffic, it may encourage pickpockets and crime, it may be dangerous, etc.

Extension idea Ask students:

- *Do you enjoy watching street performers?*
- *How much money is it reasonable to give a street performer?*
- *(if suitable) Have you ever participated in street theatre?*

Grammar

The passive

1 **Answers**
a I've been told; was only started **b** 's passed around
c they're being made a fool of **d** was taught
e we're given; you'll get moved on

2 Point out that often speakers have more than one motive for using the passive, and that the motives may be open to interpretation.

Suggested answers
2 a **3** b, d, first passive in e
4 a, b, c, d, first passive in e

3 Before doing this exercise, go through the notes in the Language reference section on page 177 (The passive) with students.

Answers
1 Our school was founded in 1904.
2 My wallet has been stolen
3 You won't be able to email me while my laptop is being repaired
4 Have you heard? I've been given a place on the course!
5 If you hadn't done the work, you would have been told off (by the teacher).

4 Remind students that, in the exam, they will get higher marks for using a range of appropriate grammar and that this includes using passives when appropriate. However, extra care needs to be taken to construct passive sentences correctly.

Answers
2 ~~going to replace~~ going to be replaced
3 ~~that is going to be read on the radio a short story by Agatha Christie~~ that a short story by Agatha Christie is going to be read on the radio
4 ~~if the computer weren't invented~~ if the computer hadn't been invented
5 ~~which has already published~~ which has already been published
6 ~~had been using~~ have been used
7 ~~nobody wants to be revealed their private life in public~~ nobody wants their private life to be revealed in public

5 Give students one minute to do this.

Answers
People go out in the open air in the early morning; they eat traditional foods; young men swim in the Nile.

6 **Answers**
1 are **2** as **3** been **4** to **5** is **6** being **7** by **8** have **9** doing **10** were (Note: *fish* can be singular or plural, depending on the context.)

7 **Answers**
1 a
2 A large number of contemporary Egyptian traditions are said to have their origins in very ancient times.
For example, offerings of fish are believed to have been made to the ancient gods ...
3 It is said that a large number of contemporary Egyptian traditions have their origins in very ancient times.
For example, it is believed that offerings of fish were made to the ancient gods.

8 Before doing this exercise, go through the notes in the Language reference section on page 177 (The passive with reporting verbs) with students.

Answers
1 It is thought that Sham el Nessím marked the start of the spring festival in ancient Egypt.
2 It is known that eating salted fish was a custom of the ancient Egyptians.
3 Five thousand people are reported to have joined in the festivities.
4 Our festival is said to have the best fireworks in the world.

9 **Answers**
1 is believed to have originated **2** expected to be chosen **3** said that the festival is **4** is thought to be **5** is considered to be **6** to go/date back more than

Extension idea Ask students to write four sentences of their own using *believe, report, say, consider, expect* or *think* in the passive.

Reading and Use of English | Part 6

1 **Answers**
1 F (There are six questions and no example.)
2 T **3** T **4** T **5** F (Read the completed text again to check it reads logically.)

2 ***As a warmer*** With books closed, ask students what they remember about Reading and Use of English Part 6, i.e. *How many questions does it have? What sort of questions are they? How should you approach the task?*

Before they start, remind them of language used for speculating about photographs – tell them to look at the Language reference section (*look, seem* and *appear*) on page 168. They then open their books and discuss the photos.

3 Give students two or three minutes to do this task.

Tell students they should do this quite carefully and take five or six minutes over it.

When they have finished, ask them to compare their ideas with their partners.

Suggested answers
Para. 2: people who attend festival; Para. 3: where the festival happens; Para. 4: the writer's arrival; Para. 5: the market; Para. 6: festival activities

4 Students should work alone to do this.

Answers
1 F **2** C **3** E **4** G **5** B **6** A

5 Once students have read the text to check their answers, ask them to work in pairs to compare their choices.

6 ***Extension idea*** Say to students: *Work in small groups. Tell each other about a strange or unusual festival in your country / this country.*

For a change of pace, you could do the photocopiable activity for this unit on the Teacher's Resources CD-ROM.

Reading and Use of English | Part 3

1 ***As a warmer*** With books closed, divide the class into two teams. Tell them that the team which calls out the correct noun for the person who does these things from each of these verbs and nouns gains a point. If they call out the wrong noun, they lose a point.

Give them an example to start off and write it on the board: *collect – collector*

You then read out the words below one by one (the correct answer is in brackets). You can give extra points if they give more than one correct answer. With words ending in *-er* and *-or*, check they know which they should use.

direct (director), *employ* (employer, employee), *work* (worker), *act* (actor/actress), *interpret* (interpreter), *translate* (translator), *visit* (visitor), *travel* (traveller), *piano* (pianist), *chemistry* (chemist), *science* (scientist), *magic* (magician), *politics* (politician)

Answers
1 tourists **2** dancers

2 EP

Answers
1 designer **2** novelist **3** researcher **4** collector **5** survivor **6** consultant **7** motorist **8** comedian **9** salesman/saleswoman/salesperson **10** specialist **11** refugee

Extension idea Ask students to work in pairs and think of one more word ending in these suffixes: *-ist, -er, -or, -ant, -ian, -man/-woman, -ee.* (Suggested answers: biologist, waiter, director, assistant, politician, policeman/policewoman, trainee)

3 **Answers**
1 eight **2** Read the whole text quickly before answering the questions **3** think what type of word you need **4** Make sure you have spelled the word correctly **5** read the completed text again

4 EP Remind students to follow the approach recommended in the Exam round-up box.

Answers
1 organisers **2** arrangements **3** activities **4** participants **5** surrounding **6** energetic **7** unusually **8** impressive

Speaking | Parts 3 and 4

1 ***As a warmer*** With books closed, tell students they are going to be working on Speaking Parts 3 and 4 in this lesson.

Ask: *How important is it to listen in the Speaking test?* (Suggested answer: You need to listen carefully to the examiner's questions; you also need to listen to what your partner is saying so that Part 3 becomes a real conversation and in Part 4 you can react to your partner's ideas and opinions.)

With books open, do the Exam round-up and discuss any issues which arise.

Answers
1 T **2** T **3** T **4** F – You should try to reach a decision, but if you don't succeed, don't worry. **5** F – It's the same subject. **6** T **7** T **8** T

2 ▶ ***Alternative treatment*** In preparation for this exercise, ask students to spend some time looking back at Units 3, 7 and 12 to remind themselves of strategies and language they can use for doing this part.

They then listen to the examiner's instructions and do the different parts of the task.

You should keep track of the time and at the end of two minutes, say 'Thank you'.

CD 2 Track 37

Examiner: I'd like you to imagine that you are going to do a class project on festivals around the world. Here are some aspects of festivals that you could investigate and a question for you to discuss. First, you have some time to look at the task. Now talk to each other about what you can learn about different places by studying these aspects of their festivals.

3 ▶ Give students one minute for this part of the task. Then round up decisions with the whole class.

CD 2 Track 38

Examiner: Now you have about a minute to decide which two aspects you and your partner should work on together.

4 ▶

CD 2 Track 39

Antonia: OK, let's see. What can we learn from studying their clothes and costumes?

Nikolai: Well, I think it shows how people carried things in the past.

Antonia: You mean, how they dressed in the past?

Nikolai: Yes, thank you, how they dressed in the past, which perhaps shows the sorts of activities they did and the materials which were available.

Antonia: That's a very good point. I think we can learn how they looked in the past, um …

Nikolai: Good, and let's move on to the food. What do you think we can learn from that?

Antonia: Um, well, I, um …

Nikolai: I mean, do you think it might show us what food was available on special occasions in the past?

Antonia: Yes, it probably does, so we learn about their past eating habits and perhaps also what they think is still important in the present.

Nikolai: Yes, that's a good idea, because of course festivals change–

Antonia: You mean they evolve.

Nikolai: Exactly, they evolve. I mean I think of festivals in my country, and the customs and traditions have changed over the years.

Antonia: An interesting point. You must have studied this a bit.

Nikolai: Yes, I have a bit. What about dances and music?

Antonia: Well, I think this is very interesting because I'm a musician myself–

Nikolai: Oh, great!

Antonia: –and I think by playing and listening to traditional festival music we learn about what is beautiful, what was lovely in the past can still be lovely for us today.

Nikolai: I think that's a very interesting general idea about all these things: that festivals really, what's the word, join the best things from the past with the best things in the present–

Antonia: In other words, combine the best things!

Nikolai: Exactly, combine the best things, so that, so that, um …

Antonia: So that, well, that's evolution, isn't it? Where the best aspects of the past and present take us on to the future.

Nikolai: Well, we're getting philosophical. I think what you're trying to explain is how we can learn about progress by looking at how festivals change, um, but what about these special activities …

5 If you did the warmer at the beginning of this section, you can omit the second half of question 1.

Ask students to note the phrases in their notebooks.

If you wish, you can print and photocopy the recording script for Track 39 from the Teacher's Resources CD-ROM for students to check their answers.

Answers

1 *Suggested answer*: They help each other with vocabulary and expressing ideas, they react to what the other person says, they invite the other person to speak and express ideas. This is important because they should try to have a normal conversation.

2 **a** That's a very good point; Yes, that's a good idea; An interesting point; I think that's a very interesting general idea …
b You mean …; In other words
c I mean …; So that (i.e. Antonia continues where Nikolai dries up.)

6 ▶ Give students two minutes to do this part of the task.

CD 2 Track 40

Examiner: I'd like you to imagine that you are doing a class project on celebrations. Here are some things people often celebrate and a question for you to discuss. First, you have some time to look at the task. Now talk to each other about how you think we should celebrate each of these occasions.

7 ▶ Give students a minute to do this part of the task.

When they have finished, round up decisions with the whole class.

CD 2 Track 41

Examiner: Now you have about a minute to decide which two occasions it would be most enjoyable to celebrate.

8 ▶ When students have finished expressing their opinions, round up ideas with the whole class.

CD 2 Track 42

Examiner: Antonia, how do towns and cities benefit from having festivals and other celebrations?

Antonia: Hmm, that's a good question. Some people say that it's good for, what's it called, community spirit, but I think the main benefit is for local businesses because tourists and visitors are attracted to the town to spend their money in shops and restaurants.

Examiner: Nikolai, do you agree with Antonia?

Nikolai: Yes, I partly agree with her. I think in many places, people spend a lot of time during the year preparing for their festival and I think it really encourages a feeling of cooperation and a community feeling.

Examiner: And, Nikolai, do you think festivals should be organised more for tourists or more for local people?

9 Pronunciation: improving fluency

This brings together several strands of pronunciation work covered during this course.

1 ▶

Answers

Hmm, ↗that's a good ↘question. / ↗Some people say that it's good for, / what's it called, / community ↘spirit, / but I think the main benefit is for local ↘businesses / because tourists and visitors are ↗attracted to the ↗town / to spend their money in shops and ↘restaurants.

CD 2 Track 43

See page 157 of the Student's Book.

2 and 3

Answers

See Pronunciation Exercise 1 above.

4 ▶

Answers

Yes, I ↗partly agree with her. / I think in ↗many places, / people spend a lot of time during the year ↗preparing for their festival / and I think it really encourages a feeling of ↘cooperation /and a ↘community feeling.

CD 2 Track 44

See page 157 of the Student's Book.

5 ***Alternative treatment*** Students have been through Antonia's and Nikolai's answers three times already, so they should be familiar with them. With books closed, ask them to give each answer with correct pronunciation from memory (they do not have to remember the exact words to do this).

If they find this too hard to do the first time, it can be done as an extension idea instead.

6 At this stage in the course, students should not need to write out their answers. Just give them a little time to prepare their ideas in their heads before they speak.

10 ***Alternative treatment*** Ask students to look back at the Speaking sections in Units 4, 8 and 12 for ideas on strategies and useful language for dealing with these questions before they start the exercise.

Extension idea When you round up, develop some of the questions into a whole-class discussion.

Writing | Part 1 An essay

1

Answers

1 140–190 words; 40 **2** you must deal with three points, one of which is your own idea **3** write a plan first **4** you should check your answer carefully when you finish

2 ***As a warmer*** With books closed, ask students, either in groups or as a whole class: *Which is better: listening to live music at a concert or music festival, or listening to recorded music?*

You can ask them about the quality of the music, how the experience is different, which is more convenient and anything else which comes up.

Once they have done the warmer, they should find the exercise in the book easier to do.

Suggested underlining
better, live, recorded music, quality, convenience, own idea

3 Give students three or four minutes to write their plans.

4 ***Alternative treatment*** Tell students to underline any useful words/phrases which they could use in their own answers. Ask them to copy these into their notebooks.

5 Tell students that punctuation, along with spelling, is one of the most frequent mistakes in the exam. Go through the Language reference section on page 177 with them and tell them to use it while they do the exercise.

Suggested answers

Although people can listen to recorded music on their music players when they are travelling, working or studying, music festivals and concerts are becoming more and more popular. This is because, I believe, they offer two main advantages.

The first advantage is that the quality of the sound is much better at live concerts, where the music and voices come directly from the performers. This makes it a much more emotional experience because you have direct contact with the musicians and you react to them and they react to you.

The second advantage is the atmosphere. Instead of listening to a recording alone on your personal music player, you are listening with a huge crowd of people and enjoying the music together. This means it is a social as well as an artistic experience.

The main disadvantage is that you cannot listen to live music whenever you want, like you can on a personal device. Apart from that, the noise from the audience sometimes spoils the quality of the sound.

In my opinion, however, the best way to enjoy music is the spontaneous atmosphere of a live concert. It is more exciting because you are surrounded by other enthusiastic fans, who are dancing with you.

6 Elicit that good referencing reduces repetition and is therefore better style.

When they have finished, go through the Language reference section on page 178 with them.

Answers

2 music festivals and concerts are becoming more and more popular
3 music festivals and concerts
4 the music and voices come directly from the performers
5 listening to music at live concerts
6 the musicians
7 you are listening with a huge crowd of people and enjoying the music together
8 The main disadvantage is that you cannot listen to live music whenever you want
9 a live concert

7 Tell students to use the Language reference section while they are doing the exercise.

Answers
1 It/This **2** it **3** they **4** they; that **5** that
6 This **7** that/this **8** that/this

Extension idea Ask students to write their own sentences using *it*, *this*, *that* and *they*. They then read them out to their groups, who should say if they have used the pronouns correctly.

If they are in doubt, they should look in the Language reference section or ask you.

8 This is the final writing task of the course and, for exam practice, should be done in about 40 minutes.

Warn students that if they spend too long on Writing Part 1 in the exam, they will not have time to deal with Part 2 adequately.

Sample answer

Films are now as popular as they were when my grandparents were young. However, now with the Internet and DVDs we have much more choice about when and where we can watch them.

There's no doubt that for the quality of the experience the best place to watch a new film is in the cinema on a wide screen with excellent sound. What is more, you can see films which everybody is talking about because they have recently been released.

The drawback of the cinema is the price of the tickets. If they were cheaper, people would go more often. This means that if, like me, you are a cinema fanatic, you have little choice but to download films off the Internet if you want to see them frequently. I also believe that it is worth seeing a good film several times. The best way of doing this is to see them first in the cinema, then later at home, when you can appreciate other aspects of the film.

For me, however, going to the cinema is a far better experience because it is a special location.

Vocabulary and grammar review Unit 13

1 **1** space **2** room **3** place **4** location **5** area **6** place **7** space **8** square **9** room **10** place

2 **1** since **2** made **3** out **4** than **5** enough **6** there **7** one **8** What

3 **1** have a tennis court built **2** you have the car checked **3** to clear up **4** have to do **5** are supposed to pay **6** are not allowed to speak

Vocabulary and grammar review Unit 14

1 **1** lawyer **2** possibilities **3** especially **4** suitably **5** responsibility **6** appropriately **7** demanding **8** representative

2 **1** reputation **2** safety **3** amazement **4** dissatisfaction **5** existence **6** truth **7** width **8** addition **9** difference **10** obligations

3 **1** is expected to arrive **2** was broken into by **3** are reported to have **4** has not / hasn't been serviced for **5** is said to be living **6** cake was / had been eaten

Writing reference

Part 1

1 **1** All young people, continue at school or college until, 18, qualifications for jobs, don't like school, own idea

2 Para. 1: should continue (my opinion)
Para. 2: jobs more specialised; more training gives more opportunities
Para. 3: many students don't enjoy school; prefer to earn money
Para. 4: uninterested students cause problems; should only study things they like after 16
Para. 5: shouldn't leave school at 16; miss opportunities

3 visit, your own country, foreign country, holiday, more interesting, cheaper, own idea

4 *Suggested answer:* The sample answer in Exercise 2 deals with each of the notes in order in separate paragraphs. This essay deals with each of the three notes in paragraph 2 with reasons for staying in your own country, and then each of the notes again in paragraph 3 with reasons for travelling abroad.

Part 2

Emails and letters

1 **1** An English friend, Pat
2 What a typical family in your country is like, and how family life is changing
3 Pat's project, different countries

2 **1** families close, spend time together, help each other, get together at weekends, young people live with parents until 25 or 30, get married in 30s, have children quite late, just one or two children
2 women now work, men take more responsibility in home, people richer, more families moving to larger houses in suburbs

Reports

1 **1** formal (It's for your teacher.)
2 The style is formal; Yes, it answers the question.

Reviews

1 **1** what it's about, why we would all enjoy it
2 everyone would enjoy, film or book
3 readers of your school's English-language magazine, i.e. other students; in the magazine

2 **1** first and second paragraphs
2 third paragraph

Articles

1 **1** g **2** d **3** e **4** h **5** c **6** b **7** a **8** i **9** f

2 Para. 1: c Para. 2: b Para. 3: a Para. 4: d

Speaking reference

2 e **3** c **4** h **5** f **6** g **7** d **8** i **9** a

Acknowledgements

This product is informed by the English Vocabulary Profile, built as part of English Profile, a collaborative programme designed to enhance the learning, teaching and assessment of English worldwide. Its main funding partners are Cambridge University Press and Cambridge Assessment and its aim is to create a 'profile' for English linked to the Common European Framework of Reference for Languages (CEF). English Profile outcomes, such as the English Vocabulary Profile, will provide detailed information about the language that learners can be expected to demonstrate at each CEF level, offering a clear benchmark for learners' proficiency. For more information, please visit www.englishprofile.org

Development of this publication has made use of the Cambridge English Corpus (CEC). The CEC is a computer database of contemporary spoken and written English, which currently stands at over one billion words. It includes British English, American English and other varieties of English. It also includes the Cambridge Learner Corpus, developed in collaboration with Cambridge Assessment. Cambridge University Press has built up the CEC to provide evidence about language use that helps to produce better language teaching materials.

Edited by Nicholas White and Catriona Watson-Brown.

Proof-read by Lucy Mordini.

Designed and typeset by Wild Apple Design Ltd.